How to Stay
Young and Healthy
in a Toxic World

Also by Ann Louise Gittleman, M.S., C.N.S.:

Beyond Pritikin
The 40/30/30 Phenomenon
Before the Change
Get the Salt Out
Get the Sugar Out
Your Body Knows Best
Super Nutrition for Women
Super Nutrition for Men
Super Nutrition for Menopause
Guess What Came to Dinner
Beyond Probiotics
Eat Fat, Lose Weight

How to Stay Young and Healthy in a Toxic World

Ann Louise Gittleman, M.S., C.N.S.

KEATS PUBLISHING

LOS ANGELES

NTC/Contemporary Publishing Group

Ann Louise Gittleman's *How to Stay Young and Healthy in a Toxic World* is not intended as medical advice. Its intent is solely informational and educational. Please consult a health professional should the need for one be indicated.

Library of Congress Cataloging-in-Publication Data

Gittleman, Ann Louise.
   How to stay young and healthy in a toxic world / Ann Louise Gittleman.
      p.   cm.
   Includes bibliographical references and index.
   ISBN 0-87983-907-4 (paper)
      1. Aging—Prevention. 2. Longevity. 3. Health. 4. Diet. 5. Toxins.
   6. Detoxification (Health)   I. Title.
   RA776.75.056 1999
   613—dc21   99-11881
                                                                   CIP

Published by Keats Publishing
A division of NTC/Contemporary Publishing Group, Inc.
4255 West Touhy Avenue, Lincolnwood (Chicago), Illinois 60646-1975 U.S.A.
Copyright © 1999 by Ann Louise Gittleman
Printed and bound in the United States of America
International Standard Book Number: 0-87983-907-4
10 9 8 7 6 5 4 3 2 1

*To Evelyn Gregan and Inge Baer
who were always there for me
from the very beginning*

Contents

Acknowledgments

My special thanks to:

- Norman Goldfind for his belief in this project. I am most grateful to him for understanding the importance of detoxification to health and healing.
- My editors Phyllis Herman and Peter Hoffman for their patience, understanding and guidance.
- Marcia Bragg, whose unfailing grace under extreme pressure made this book possible.

I am also appreciative of the expert advice provided by water expert Dr. Roy Speiser and light expert Dr. Brian Breiling. The support provided by the Parcells Center, especially Joseph Dispenza, was most gratifying. My thanks to Stuart K. Gittleman, Director of Operations at ALG, Inc., who kept our operation afloat while this manuscript was created. Thanks also to Sherri Boylan who assisted me on a personal and professional level throughout. Last but not least, I am grateful for the help of my technical support expert, Jon Weidenaar.

1
A New View of Aging

*"If you want to be healthy, you have to trade your wishbone for
a backbone and get to work!"*

—DR. HAZEL PARCELLS

A healthy body is a clean body. Yet, as we approach the millennium, a clean body is becoming virtually unattainable. Toxins are all around us, hiding in the food we eat, the environment and even created by our body's own metabolic processes. Thus, our immune systems weaken and we grow old before our time, gaining weight and becoming vulnerable to heart disease, cancer and a host of autoimmune disorders.

The most widely accepted theory of aging today is that it is caused by oxidative stress. Oxidative stress or free radicals (also known as reactive oxygen molecules) damage our cells and tissues by weakening and altering cellular membranes which allow bacteria and viruses to enter the body. In addition, free radical damage destroys genetic coding, resulting in cellular chaos that leads to deteriorating changes in all of our tissues and organs, including the brain.

Free radicals come from a variety of sources, including heavy metals, radiation, pollution, preservatives and stress, but also from normal metabolism and even the process of detoxification itself. Most approaches to fighting free radicals focus only on controlling their devastating effects by neutralizing their reactions with high doses of antioxidants like superoxide dismutase, catalase and glutathione peroxidase as well as vitamins A, C and E. Yet the most toxic underlying causes of free radical proliferation—sugar, parasites, heavy metals and radiation—are often ignored. I believe that these four toxic invaders depress the immune system and cause disease and premature aging.

In this book, I will identify the most prevalent toxic invaders of our time and, most importantly, I will show you how to eliminate them from your life with a special detox program and natural prescriptions for safe alternatives.

But before we begin, let's take a good, hard look at the challenge 21st century living presents to us. Today, more than ever before, our bodies are being bombarded by an array of pesticides, chemicals, environmental pollutants, heavy metals and parasites that is truly mind-boggling. Consider these 1989 statistics:

- 551,034,696 pounds of industrial chemicals were dumped into public sewage storage.
- 1,180,831,181 pounds of chemicals were released into the ground, threatening our natural aquifers.
- 188,953,884 pounds of chemicals were discharged into surface waters.
- 2,427,061,906 pounds of air emissions were pumped into the atmosphere.

Toxins enter our systems through our food, air and water, and the accumulation of toxins in the environment over the past 50 years has made our bodies an ever-expanding toxic waste dump.

Every single day we are exposed to poisons knowingly and un-knowingly. A whole new breed of foreign chemicals called xeno-biotics has been introduced into the environment since World War II, adding 50 different varieties of synthetic estrogens and estrogen-disruptors to our chemical soup.

Stone-age Bodies

Almost like characters in a science fiction novel, we Americans and people in other developed countries have left our bodies be-hind as we move forward into the technological future. Our di-gestive systems, our bodies' absorption of nutrients and our metabolisms are all adapted to the natural foods of preindustrial times. Our bodies have not evolved in pace with technological change. They have been left behind. They do not have enzymes and metabolic pathways to break down many of today's artificial foods into harmless by-products. Our bodies don't function as well on factory-made foods as on those designed by Mother Na-ture. Bad things happen. Symptoms appear. We may be given ar-tificial drugs—and even artificial organs—to cure the symptoms caused by artificial food.

The good news is that our bodies were designed with a complex and sophisticated detoxification system. Made up of the skin, lungs, liver, kidneys, blood, bowels and lymph, the detox system is ca-pable of working with a precision not duplicated in any of man's inventions. The bad news is that in addition to eliminating the breakdown products that result from normal metabolic processes, this system has now been forced to rid the body of heavy metals and toxic chemicals like drugs, alcohol, pesticides, herbicides and food additives. And we make it work even harder because of our sedentary lifestyles, our fast-food diets and our stressed-out lives.

Our 21st century lifestyle can often overwhelm our biological design. When this happens, we experience any number of devastating symptoms. Toxic bodies produce tired people who are often tense and irritable. We may suffer from headaches, insomnia, depression, allergies, poor digestion, bad breath or skin problems. Long-term toxic overload can lead to immune suppression and possibly chronic illness like arthritis, cancer and Alzheimer's disease.

In Chapters 7 and 8, I will introduce you to some very effective cleansing programs that will not only help lighten your body's load but will rid you of excess weight and make you look and feel young again.

Are Environmental Health Problems All in the Mind?

Emotions also play an important role in our health. In his book *When the Body Speaks Its Mind,* New York psychiatrist Berney Goodman describes how we all, quite normally, react to emotional stress with physical symptoms. Dr. Goodman calls this *somatization* and says that it occurs when we express our feelings of distress through physical symptoms rather than words. He says that 60 to 80 percent of Americans have at least one somatization symptom a week, such as feeling lower back pain after a stressful day of office work. Is it possible, then, that at least some of the symptoms that we blame on environmental causes are really caused by stress, depression or some other emotion? Very possibly, yes.

Assuming that a certain amount of worry about the environment and our health is no more than worry, are there a sufficient number of dangerous ecological developments to arouse concern in a reasonably objective observer? Large numbers of unbiased people already think that there are. As natural balances are interfered with and environmental illness becomes more widespread, it becomes increasingly harder to calm and reassure the public. Some people in government would like to take action about these growing environmental problems, but they are prevented from doing so by the vested interests that fund political campaigns. For the foreseeable future, environmentally aware Americans will have to look out for themselves and those they care about.

Disaster Scenarios

Unlike natural disasters like fires, tornadoes, floods and outbreaks of communicable disease, environmental disasters belong in a class by themselves. They involve not only uncontrollable natural forces but human miscalculation. The marriage between human miscalculation and uncontrollable natural forces can be grand in scale and played out over a period of time. In fact, the largeness or complexity of the problem and the relatively slow rate of its build-up have often caused us to miss what was going on until the situation was far advanced.

In 1962, Rachel Carson's book *Silent Spring* first sounded the alarm to a passive public about the potential hazards of synthetic pesticides, especially DDT. Hailed as one of the landmark books of the 20th century which altered the course of history, Carson's book revolutionized environmental laws affecting our land, air and water. It also forced the banning of DDT and launched the environmental movement. Thirty-six years later, other pesticides continue to threaten our health.

In the same way that symptoms reveal the presence of an

underlying illness, environmental disasters reveal the presence of an underlying conflict between human beings and the natural world. Where one disaster occurs, others with a similar cause are sure to follow. The conflicts between humans and nature are grand in scale in America and have been building up since the Industrial Age began.

In her recent book *Natural Acts,* ecologist Amy Dean related the following story about professional golfer Damacio Lopez who retired to his hometown of Socorro, New Mexico after having been away for many years. When he began to hear loud explosions, followed by smoke drifting through town and into people's homes, nobody could explain what was going on. Eventually, Lopez discovered, to his distress, that uranium munitions were being batch-tested nearby and that the smoke drifting into his and his neighbors' homes was radioactive. This was in the mid-1980s, so no one involved in the testing could plead ignorance to the health risks to which they were exposing families.

Dean also recounts how a 1978 flood in the Southern Californian rural community of Glen Avon released an acrid smell in the air and a strange foam floated on water that collected in puddles throughout town. The local kids splashed in the water and used the foam to make mock beards on their faces. Only when the children's jeans and sneakers fell apart and their noses bled did parents become concerned. Some children developed double vision, severe headaches or red, irritated skin. It turned out that in this rural corner a hazardous waste dump had been hidden since 1955 in a box canyon less than a mile away from the elementary school. The 17-acre site held more than 34 million gallons of waste chemicals. Heavy rains and subsequent floodgates brought a toxic solution into town streets and backyards.

Both of these incidents galvanized the local people into political activity. Yet these people did not see themselves as environmentalists or indeed as activists of any sort. If it hadn't happened to them, they would have done nothing. This describes the attitude of most of us. Until something really hits home, we are passive observers.

Radioactive Waste

Perhaps the passivity of Americans about public health and environmental threats is due to our wishful assumption that some government authority must be monitoring things and watching out so that no harm befalls us. The following story, from a recent *New York Times* report, illustrates quite the contrary.

Half of all the uranium ever mined is now stored in three waste dumps in the American heartland. The waste consists of depleted radioactive uranium from nuclear bombs, power plants and submarine reactors. About 1.25 billion pounds of it are stored in 14-ton steel cylinders. There are 28,351 cylinders at Paducah, Kentucky, 13,388 at Piketon, Ohio and 4,683 at Oak Ridge, Tennessee. They are all exposed to the weather, and some are heavily coated with rust. If moisture gets inside a cylinder, it causes a heat-generating reaction that releases a toxic white gas. The word *big* hardly describes the size of this problem.

Yet these uranium dumps have a low priority in comparison with the government's even larger problems. Among these are the millions of gallons of radioactive and toxic liquids in leaking or earthquake-vulnerable tanks in South Carolina and Washington state. The Portsmouth Gaseous Diffusion Plant, south of Columbus, Ohio, is another top-priority problem, having already contaminated the groundwater with radioactive uranium.

The government has come up with a bureaucratic solution to the problem of the three huge dumps of spent uranium in steel drums. The spent uranium is simply classified as source material, i.e. fuel, instead of waste. Therefore, legally, nothing needs to be done about it except to scrape off the rust and repaint the drums occasionally. Had the depleted uranium been classified as waste, federal law would have required that it be disposed of, at a possible cost of millions of dollars to the government. But experts can't agree about what to do with radioactive waste, in any case.

The Cell from Hell

I don't want to give the impression that all scientists and administrators are inactive in protecting environment-related public health. That would be far from the truth. But I think it's fair to say that those individuals who do make progress in this area have to swim very strongly against the current. Yet the efforts of these few do reward the many.

Aquatic ecologist JoAnn Burkholder, of North Carolina State University, is one of the people who has insisted on the truth becoming known. Her struggle with state authorities is told in the recent book *And the Waters Turned to Blood* by Rodney Barker. In North Carolina river estuaries, she discovered *Pfiesteria piscida,* a new organism in the group that causes red and brown tides. Her discovery came about when she tried to find out what was killing a colleague's research fish. This organism cripples rivers with massive fish kills. Both the Pamlico and Neuse estuaries in North Carolina have been devastated by multiple fish kills. Burkholder found out the hard way that this organism's toxins affect people as well as fish. In her lab, she breathed in fumes from fish dying of *Pfiesteria* infection and developed burning eyes, cramps and nausea. Then she couldn't remember phone numbers or even what she had just said in a conversation. She got over her symptoms quickly, but a research aide took months to recover from a similar exposure. Three years later, both still had occasional lingering symptoms.

Where did this "cell from hell," as it has been called, come from so suddenly? Such organisms probably have always existed in small numbers from Delaware to the Gulf of Mexico, but something in North Carolina rivers permitted the organism to bloom in huge numbers and kill off fish. That "something," Burkholder showed, was runoff into rivers from huge new hog farms upstream. Neither the big agribusinesses that own the hog farms nor the state authorities supposed to supervise them were pleased to hear this. In 1994, the director of the state's water quality program was alleged to have scrawled an obscenity on cleanup recommendations submitted to him. More recently, 70 North Carolina doctors achieved a one-year moratorium on new hog farms in three counties because of festering sores that the organism caused on humans. Although there was a 25-million-gallon spill of hog manure into North Carolina coastal waters in 1994, Deborah Atwood, a vice president of the National Pork Producers Council, claimed that state controls were too strict and that city pollution and global warming were responsible for *Pfiesteria.*

Outbreaks of *Pfiesteria* occurred in four rivers emptying into the Chesapeake Bay in August and September 1997. "There is no problem as we see it right now," said Kay Richardson, president of Delmarva Poultry Industry Inc., a trade association of about 4,000 chicken farmers. Don Boesch, an oceanographer at the University of Maryland, believes that runoff from poultry farms is a likely cause of *Pfiesteria* outbreaks. He said that agricultural manure runoff is also a probable cause of algal blooms that cause "dead zones" in the sea. According to him, there is already a small dead zone at the bottom of Chesapeake Bay, and another the size of New Jersey in the Gulf of Mexico.

Detoxify, Don't Retoxify

I hope that these frightening examples will help convince you that environmental degradation—and the health threats involved— is underway at a pace unimaginable a few decades ago, when Rachel Carson wrote *Silent Spring.* One great difference is that present-day environmental health threats are unlikely to be as straightforward and visible as smoke belching from a factory chimney, though there are still plenty of those around. As our technology grows more complex in leaps and bounds, nature's responses are growing harder even for experts to read. But it's clear that we don't fully understand all the health consequences when we make tradeoffs of large-scale destruction of natural resources for immediate industrial rewards. We severely underestimate Mother Nature. She probably has many more unpredictable responses in store for us, along the lines of Burkholder's organism, which lay nearly dormant until it was roused by a change in natural balances.

You don't have to be an ecologist or an environmental activist to protect your family and yourself from what is happening all around you. All you need to do is become aware of hidden dangers where you live and work—and then minimize any negative effects through lifestyle changes and nutritional support. As with stress, it's almost impossible to avoid environmental toxins in today's world. As with stress, you first have to learn how to locate the sources of toxicity and then learn how to manage them.

Once you detoxify your body, be careful not to retoxify it. Or, perhaps more realistically, take control where you can, particularly in the foods you choose to eat, the water you choose to drink and in the quality of your indoor air and light. Nutrition and knowledge are the keys. Organic, properly cleansed food remains the most effective medicine available. Becoming aware is the first step needed to protect and control your health.

How This Book Can Help

We will start our journey to a healthier, slimmer body, less prone to disease and premature aging, by looking in detail at the four greatest hidden threats to health in America today.

1. **Sugar** robs us of a healthy immune system and a normal resistance to disease. Studies show that sugar in any form is a potent suppressor of the immune system and is implicated in over 60 ailments ranging from heart disease to various forms of cancer. In fact, cancer thrives on sugar. Just 3½ ounces of sugar (even in natural forms like fruit juice or excess fruit) suppresses the germicidal ability of white blood cells up to five hours after consumption.

2. **Parasites** may well be the most immunosuppressive (and therefore aging) invader of all in the body. Today, over 50 percent of all Americans will test positive for one or more "uninvited" guests. The tiny parasite *cryptosporidium* is now considered a serious threat and has been found in practically every water system in the country. This and other microscopic vampires have been connected to chronic fatigue, allergy, irritable bowel syndrome and a lowered resistance to disease.

3. **Heavy metals** such as lead, mercury, aluminum and copper are generally recognized as body pollutants. What is not recognized is that three of these metals are commonly used dental materials in the mouth where they can be very immunoreactant. Mercury has been linked to depression, lupus, multiple sclerosis, ringing in the ears and unexplained skin conditions. Aluminum has been connected to premature senility, mental disorientation, constipation and severe dryness of the tissues and mucous membranes. Copper has been linked to panic attacks, hyperactivity and hair and nail breakdown.

4. **Radiation** from x-rays, nuclear plants, bomb fallout and travel on airplanes may cause the kind of tiredness that no amount of sleep seems to relieve as well as glandular weakness and the inability to heal. Radiation particles displace vital minerals in the system.

Then, we will look at the health risks found in the ordinary indoor home environment. There are many. Besides radon, household chemicals and formaldehyde which you may already have been alerted to, did you realize that wall-to-wall synthetic carpeting is one of the more dangerous things you can bring into your house or apartment? And that artificial lighting inside your home may be a major contributory cause to seasonal affective disorder (SAD)? An extensive checklist in Chapter 8 will enable you to take an inventory of the potential dangers in your own home.

Next, we consider our water supply. How can we be sure that the water we drink is pure? The term *pure,* when applied to water, has specific meanings and much significance for our health. If your own water source is questionable, I will tell you how to filter out the impurities. Continuing the search for purity, I suggest a number of ways to purify your food as well as tell you what you need to watch out for like irradiation, microwaves and the dangers of genetically engineered foods.

My personal detoxification plan, starting with the Detox 'n Diet program, shows you how to flush such toxins from your system by supporting the function of your liver, the key detoxifying organ, through special foods (including proteins and oils) as well as liver-supporting supplementation. Detox 'n Diet can be used as a stand-alone detox program or as a transitional program for better overall eating.

The detoxification program will follow with some more of my favorite ways to detox, which can be done individually or in conjunction with the Detox 'n Diet. You will learn how to apply a castor oil pack to the abdomen to assist the liver and gall bladder to release physical and emotional toxins, and I will teach you how to do the widely acclaimed coffee enema. I will also share with you my favorite Bach flower remedies that are outstanding for unbalanced emotional states. I consider the Bach flower remedies to be a kind of noninvasive psychotherapy in a bottle. I am sure you will feel the same way when you start using them.

It is true that we currently live in a risky environment. But we can detoxify our bodies and, with a little effort, live free of the ill effects of modern technology. I am constantly working at it. I have written this book in the hope that you will join me.

2
Toxic Invaders Questionnaire

Identifying your personal health invaders, like sugar, parasites, heavy metals and/or radiation, is the first step in your personal plan for growing younger now. So let's begin the journey to a longer, more youthful life by taking a moment to fill out the Toxic Invader Questionnaire. This questionnaire is actually a lifestyle checklist which will help you to pinpoint your personal health invaders that will need to be further investigated in your quest to stay young and healthy in a toxic world. This questionnaire can also be used to give you a quick sense of which chapters are most important for you.

Sugar	Yes	No
Do you fill your cupboards—and your body—with "fat free" and low-fat baked goods?	___	___
Are you more conscious of counting fat grams than sugar grams?	___	___
Do you usually crave something sweet after a meal?	___	___
Do you drink a lot of fruit juice, thinking it is better than soda?	___	___

	Yes	No
Do you eat more than five pieces of fruit a day?	___	___
Do you drink more than two sweetened sodas per day?	___	___
Have you always had a sweet tooth?	___	___

Parasites

	Yes	No
Have you ever traveled to Mexico, Africa, Israel, China, Russia, Asia, Europe or to Central or South America?	___	___
Have you had intestinal problems, unexplained fever, night sweats or an elevated white blood count since traveling?	___	___
Is your water supply from a mountainous area?	___	___
Do you drink untested well water?	___	___
Do you backpack and drink from pristine-looking lakes and streams?	___	___
Do you eat sushi or raw or undercooked fish or meat?	___	___
Do you frequently eat in restaurants or purchase prepared foods from salad bars or delicatessens?	___	___
At home, do you use the same cutting board for chicken, fish and meat as you do for vegetables?	___	___
Have you ever had a pet?	___	___
Do you work at a day-care center?	___	___

Heavy Metals	Yes	No
Do you take antacids?	___	___
Do you use aluminum pots and pans for cooking?	___	___
Do you live in a home built in the 1930s?	___	___
Do you have mercury amalgam fillings or porcelain crowns in your teeth?	___	___
Do you currently have or have you ever had a copper IUD?	___	___
Do you work in an industrial plant or have hobbies in which you come in contact with heavy metals?	___	___
Do you eat off of unglazed ceramic dishes?	___	___

Radiation

	Yes	No
Do you fly more than four times a year?	___	___
Do you live in New York, Colorado, Illinois, Massachusetts, New Jersey, Ohio, Pennsylvania, Connecticut, Florida or South Carolina (states with heavy nuclear plants)?	___	___
Have you ever undergone radiation treatment?	___	___

Indoor Air Environment

	Yes	No
Do you live in an area with high radon?	___	___
Do you or does someone in your family smoke indoors?	___	___

	Yes	No
Do you have a newly installed synthetic carpet?	____	____
Do you use a lot of commercial cleaning products in your home?	____	____
Do you use a humidifier?	____	____
Do you use permanent-pressed sheets?	____	____
Do you live in a mobile home?	____	____
Do you often notice mold around the tiles and pipes?	____	____
Do you have an unvented gas stove?	____	____
Do you have pressed wood cabinets or furniture?	____	____

Indoor Light Environment

	Yes	No
Do you spend most of the time indoors?	____	____
Do you feel depressed during the late fall or early winter?	____	____
Do you have artificial fluorescent lights?	____	____

Water

	Yes	No
Do you drink unfiltered water?	____	____
Do you take a lot of baths and showers?	____	____
Do you drink tap water?	____	____
Do you drink well water?	____	____
Do you drink water bottled in plastic containers?	____	____
Is your water hard with calcium deposits?	____	____
Have nitrates been found in your water supply?	____	____

	Yes	No
Have parasites like cryptosporidum or giardia been found in your water supply?	——	——

Food

	Yes	No
Do you often eat nonorganic strawberries or cherries?	——	——
Do you eat a lot of fast foods?	——	——
Do you eat out in restaurants frequently?	——	——
Do you consume irradiated foods like poultry, potatoes, meat or spices?	——	——
Do you buy your produce, meat and dairy foods from the supermarket?	——	——
Do you eat genetically engineered foods?	——	——
Do you use a microwave?	——	——

Of course, the more items you have checked off with a "yes" in the questionnaire, the greater your toxic burden. You have already taken a giant step in your journey to reversing the aging process by simply becoming aware of your personal health invaders. Now that you have identified which toxins in your life need further investigation, you can proceed through the book and learn how to minimize their effects and eliminate them from your life as much as possible. The special detoxification program presented later in this book, the Detox 'n Diet, will significantly help you to detoxify from the inside out.

3
Sugar:
Toxic Invader #1

Despite what the mainstream media would like us to believe, sugar is not an innocent substance that gives us pleasure and causes no harm. Quite the contrary, I can think of nothing in the diet that promotes disease and aging more over the long term than excess sugar. The scientific evidence I have seen for the past 20 years has lead me to the inescapable conclusion that sugar is truly a dietary demon. The "sugar is bad for our health" message was lost during the media demonization of fats during the 1980s and early '90s. But now it's high time to resurrect this important message and understand why eliminating sugar will help keep us young and vital.

Believe it or not, there are over 60 ailments that have been associated with sugar consumption in the medical literature. They include the following:

Addiction (drugs, caffeine, food)	Alcoholism	Asthma
	Allergies	Behavior problems
Adrenal gland exhaustion	Anxiety	Binge eating
	Appendicitis	Bloating
Aging and wrinkling, premature	Arthritis	Bone loss

Cancer

Candidiasis

Cataracts

Cholesterol, high LDL

Colitis

Concentration difficulties

Constipation

Depression

Dermatitis

Diabetes

Digestion, impaired

Diverticulitis

Diverticulosis

Eczema

Edema

Emotional problems

Endocrine gland dysfunction

Estrogen levels, high

Fatigue

Food cravings

Gallstones

Gastric overacidity

Gout

HDL cholesterol, low

Heart disease

Hormonal problems

Hyperactivity

Hypertension

Hypoglycemia

Immunity, weakened

Impotence

Indigestion

Insomnia

Kidney stones

Liver dysfunction

Menstrual difficulties

Mental illness

Mood swings

Muscle pain

Nearsightedness

Obesity

Osteoporosis

Parasitic infection

Premenstrual syndrome

Psoriasis

Rheumatism

Tooth decay

Triglyceride levels, high

Ulcers

Vaginal yeast infections

Too New for Comfort

Have you ever considered the fact that almost all of the degenerative diseases that plague us today were practically nonexistent just 200 years ago? According to a 1912 *Journal of the American*

Medical Association article, cardiovascular disease, for example, was so rare that research wasn't even conducted on it until 1912— and that first study examined only four cases! So what has changed so dramatically between then and now to bring on devastating conditions like cardiovascular disease?

Without a doubt, the biggest change in our diets has been our sugar consumption. Yes, sugar, in the form of the refined white sugar known as sucrose, brown sugar, corn sweeteners, high fructose corn syrup, dextrose, glucose, lactose and maltose. Unfortunately, our bodies didn't have a chance to gradually adapt to this relatively new substance in our diets. Over the past two centuries, we have literally shocked our bodily systems with outrageous and ever-growing amounts of nutrient-robbing sugar. The statistics speak for themselves. According to Dr. James Scala, at the end of the 1700s sugar consumption was less than 20 pounds per person per year. By the end of the 1800s, sugar consumption had risen to 63 pounds annually. Now, 100 years later, the average American eats 152 pounds of sugar each year.

The Sugar Disease Connection

As sugar consumption has risen, so too has the incidence of degenerative health problems. This pattern has been observed not only in the United States but in every society studied. Half a century ago, researcher Weston A. Price observed countless cultures from the Arctic to the tropics and noted that physical degeneration and diseases developed in those societies over a period of a single generation once refined sugary carbohydrates were added to the diets.

In the 1970s, British Surgeon Captain T. L. Cleave conducted another classic study in which he found that increases in degenerative conditions like diabetes, hypertension and heart disease all could be traced to increases in refined carbohydrate intake. In every case, Cleave found that primitive cultures were almost entirely free of these diseases until about 20 years after white sugar and white flour were introduced. While the addition of sugar to the diets of nonindustrialized societies didn't seem to cause health problems immediately, Cleave observed that it always caused health problems like heart disease and diabetes to begin about two decades later. This pattern was so consistent in all the cultures Cleave studied that he named the phenomenon the "Rule of 20 Years."

British researcher John Yudkin, M.D., also saw the sugar connection to disease. He conducted numerous studies on this subject and eventually found that sugar was a more likely cause of heart disease than fat. The results of his studies in the 1970s led Yudkin to warn that feeding children so much sugar lays the foundation for the development of serious diseases in the future and may even be as hazardous to their long-term health as smoking.

The unheeded warnings of these pioneering researchers unfortunately seem to be coming true. With our sugar consumption at an all-time high, so is the incidence of cardiovascular disease (CVD). According to recent estimates by the American Heart Association, 60 million Americans now have some type of CVD, and the disease took the lives of approximately one million people in 1993. Remember, CVD was unheard of in the 18th century.

The Role of Insulin in Disease

Although researchers have seen a correlation between sugar intake and the incidence of heart disease and diabetes for decades, we now have a much better understanding of why sugar contributes to ill health. It has to do with the hormone, insulin.

Secreted by the pancreas when sugar or other carbohydrates are eaten, insulin is designed to maintain blood sugar balance by causing excess sugar to be removed from the bloodstream and moved either into muscle glycogen for energy or into fat storage. This mechanism is part of the body's normal function, but the body was never designed to cope with the forms and amounts of sugar we have available today. White sugar and overly sweetened foods of any type cause concentrated sugars to flood the bloodstream, and the body responds by raising insulin levels very high and very fast.

What kind of effect does consistently high insulin (hyperinsulinemia) have on the body? It causes an increase in cholesterol production and fat storage and it also is linked to hypertension. Many researchers think high insulin is the major underlying cause of these conditions. Insulin expert Ralph DeFronzo, M.D., of the University of Texas Health Center, uses the metaphor of an iceberg with its tips exposed, to describe hyperinsulinemia. During meetings and speeches, DeFronzo draws a picture of a huge iceberg with peaks labeled High Cholesterol, Hypertension, Heart Disease, Diabetes and Obesity—conditions that are part of a growing disorder known in some medical circles as Syndrome X.

Although DeFronzo's "peaks" are visible above the water in the representation, there's a great dangerous mass that lies hidden beneath the surface and DeFronzo labels that mass "hyperinsulinemia." In DeFronzo's mind, high blood pressure, high cholesterol and obesity are not really diseases at all but are "symptoms" or indications of the underlying disease of hyperinsulinemia. Patients notice the indicators, and doctors try to solve each condition individually, but researchers like DeFronzo see hyperinsulinemia as the root cause that needs to be treated or, ideally, prevented. Insulin resistance, which seems to go hand in hand with hyperinsulinemia, is a condition in which receptors in the cells no longer respond properly to insulin.

Hyperinsulinemia also appears to be involved in cancer. According to researcher Barry Sears, Ph.D., author of *The Zone,* cancer is a condition that is associated with the runaway production of bad hormonelike substances called eicosanoids, and high insulin levels cause the production of eicosanoids. Eicosanoids not only suppress immune function so that the body can't fight cancer, but they also keep cancer cells growing and promote the spread of cancer throughout the body.

Breast cancer, for one, has been associated with high insulin levels. Writing in the *Annals of the New York Academy of Science,* internationally acclaimed scientist Dr. Vladimir Dilman showed that breast cancer patients have insulin levels that are 22 percent higher than healthy controls. Patrick Quillin, Ph.D., R.D., C.N.S., an expert on nutrition for cancer, also has warned about the dangers of high sugar intake and high blood insulin levels. "Elevating blood glucose in a cancer patient is like throwing gasoline on a smoldering fire," he writes in his book *Beating Cancer with Nutrition.*

The Detrimental Effects of Sugar on Children

The evidence indicates that the key to preventing diseases like cancer, heart disease and diabetes is to discourage blood sugar spikes and overproduction of insulin. This is as important for kids as it is for adults. Although it's easy for us to think sugar won't harm children because their blood sugar–balancing systems tend to work so well, the consumption of unprecedented amounts of sugar is wreaking havoc on the health of today's children. The percentage of teenage children who are overweight, for example, has increased from 15 percent in the 1970s to 21 percent in 1991.

Insulin-induced hormonal difficulties also are increasing in teenagers. Diana Schwarzbein, M.D., head of the Endocrinology Institute of Santa Barbara, has commented on the growing number of hormonal problems she sees in teenage girls who have been brought up on a high-carbohydrate diet loaded with sugar. According to Schwarzbein, common complaints of teenage girls today include acne, premenstrual syndrome, painful periods and excess facial hair—all symptoms that are side effects caused from too much sugar and carbohydrates in the diet. Carbohydrates increase insulin secretion, and insulin in turn causes the adrenal gland to secrete androgens such as testosterone, which disturb normal female hormonal functioning.

When children overindulge in sugar, the development of hyperinsulinemia and insulin resistance is accelerated as well as the serious health problems associated with these conditions. Although it seems as though children can guzzle down sugar-sweetened foods and soft drinks without paying the price, don't be fooled, say family medicine and weight-loss specialists Drs. Michael and Mary Dan Eades. Poor diet and genes eventually do catch up with children's more finely tuned blood sugar–regulating mechanisms. The two doctors explain this in their recent book *Protein Power:*

> When you're a kid . . . the pancreas releases just a small amount of insulin to force the blood sugar back down to normal because in childhood the cells are extremely sensitive to insulin. Small amounts of insulin translate into low insulin levels. And due to this delicate sensitivity, small amounts of insulin easily can handle even the outrageous amounts of sugar and other carbohydrates that kids stuff themselves with—but not without a price. That price is a developing loss

of sensitivity of the sensors to insulin—a condition known as insulin resistance—and chronically elevated insulin levels. And all the disorders (obesity, high cholesterol, hypertension, heart disease and diabetes) that eventually follow.

Although the media would like you to believe otherwise, preventing children from overindulging in sweets is one of the most loving and health-promoting things you can do for them. It's also one of the most healthful things you can do for yourself. Because of the far-reaching health problems associated with excess sugar intake, I consider knowing how to reduce sugar in the diet an essential survival skill for slowing down the aging process.

Sugar Impairs Immunity

Sugar functions in the body as an immunosuppressant. In other words, it suppresses our immune system, which protects us from viruses, bacteria and other invaders. With the increasing incidence of viral, bacterial and parasite epidemics, many due to increased international travel and relaxed sexual mores, we need the protection of our immune system more than ever today.

Sugar affects the immune system in the following ways:

- It lessens the germ-killing ability of white blood cells for up to five hours.
- It interferes with the production of antibodies, which attack invaders in the bloodstream.
- It disrupts the distribution of vitamin C, one of the body's most important antioxidants.
- It causes mineral imbalances that weaken the immune system and are sometimes responsible for allergic reactions. Sugar is also one of the top seven food allergens.

- By neutralizing the action of essential fatty acids, it makes cell walls more permeable and therefore easier for invaders to penetrate.

Sugar has long been known to cause dental cavities, but recent medical research has revealed that sugar is also associated with much more serious conditions such as cancer, heart disease, high blood pressure and weakened immunity. Additionally, the excess calories derived from sugar in food are stored as body fat in much the same way as excess calories from saturated fat are.

Today, we are warned about fat and sodium, but someday I foresee that food packages will also carry prominent warnings of sugar's risks. This is no exaggeration. In fact, refined sugar acts more like a drug in our bodies than a nutrient. Sugar has no nutrients—only calories—and the body has to use its own mineral reserves to digest it. For this reason, a high-sugar diet can paradoxically cause obesity and malnutrition at the same time.

Sugar and Degenerative Diseases

To sum up, I have labeled sugar as the number-one toxic invader for the following reasons:

- Heart disease, adult-onset diabetes and cancer, three of our country's most common and feared killers, are continuing to rise at alarming numbers.
- Obesity in America is at an all-time high, affecting one in every three people in this country.
- A growing percentage of the American population is now developing insulin resistance, a condition that is linked to many serious problems including high blood pressure, high cholesterol levels, heart disease, obesity and adult-onset diabetes.

Research shows that there is a common factor that is implicated in the development of all of these seemingly unrelated health problems. It's something few would suspect. It's spelled S-U-G-A-R.

What About Artificial Sweeteners?

The only good thing you can say for artificial sweeteners is that they do not cause tooth decay. Except in the case of people who drink large amounts of soft drinks, sugar substitutes may not even result in a reduction of calories ingested. This is because they may actually increase the body's craving for sweets as well as fats. In other words, they make it harder to kick the sugar habit.

In the decade or so since artificial sweeteners have become widely used by Americans, our sugar consumption has increased by more than 10 percent and we have become 30 percent fatter.

Aspartame. Sold under the brand names of NutraSweet and Equal, aspartame is the most widely used artificial sweetener in soft drinks and dietetic foods. It is about 180 times sweeter than white sugar. People with phenylketonuria (PKU) are warned not to use it because aspartame breaks down to phenylalanine, a compound they must avoid. For everyone, phenylalanine interferes with production of the neurotransmitter serotonin; this can result in a range of symptoms from depression to premenstrual syndrome. Too little serotonin can also cause cravings for sugar and carbohydrates and thus may be responsible for binge eating.

The Aspartame Consumer Safety Network reported that 75 percent of all nondrug complaints to the Food and Drug Administration involve aspartame. Its use has been blamed for five deaths and at least 70 symptoms. Dr. Russell Blaylock, in his book *Excitotoxins: The Taste That Kills,* claims that aspartame damages neurons and is a health risk for Alzheimer's disease and other nervous system disorders. Doctors at the Harvard Medical School have warned that children may be especially vulnerable to aspartame for two reasons: (1) their smaller body weight makes the dose relatively more harmful; and (2) over their lifetimes, they will be exposed to aspartame for much longer than present adults.

Saccharin and cyclamate. These have proven to be carcinogenic to experimental animals and should never be used. In late 1997, questions were raised about the validity of regarding saccharin as a carcinogen. While saccharin caused bladder tumors in rats, reasons have been offered to show that these results do not apply to humans. However, on October 31, 1997, a federal advisory panel to the National Toxicology Program of the National Institutes of Health voted 4–3 to keep saccharin listed as a carcinogen. Even if that recommendation is not accepted and saccharin is declared noncarcinogenic, it will remain a high-risk and unsafe substance in the opinion of many prominent nutritionists and researchers.

Sorbitol, mannitol, xylitol and hydrogenated starch hydrolysate. Classified as sugar alcohols, these artificial sweeteners are noncaloric because they are more or less indigestible. However, they can be broken down by some intestinal bacteria and can result in diarrhea and cramps. Xylitol has been shown to cause tumors and organ damage in animals. In his book *No More Cravings,* Dr. Douglas Hunt claims that, like sugar, sugar alcohols can increase hunger and cause allergies. Sorbitol and mannitol are often found in sugar-free chewing gum.

Author-physician Isadore Rosenfeld recently mentioned two interesting cases. A flight attendant went to a clinic about her problems with diarrhea which she had been having for seven years and which had been diagnosed as irritable bowel syndrome. The clinic doctors found nothing wrong with her. They noticed in her medical history that she chewed 60 sticks of sugar-free gum a day. These contained a total of 75 grams of sorbitol, which traveled undigested through her intestines and emerged with water as diarrhea. That case reminded Rosenfeld of a patient of his own, a 47-year-old woman with four years of complaints of a nervous stomach. He would not have made the right diagnosis had he not noticed her frequently sucking mints. A single mint can contain up to 2 grams of sorbitol, so that sucking only five or six a day can cause gastric problems and diarrhea.

Acesulfame potassium. The Center for Science in the Public Interest has warned that this sweetener, sold under the brand name of Sunette, may be a carcinogen.

Added to the undesirable qualities of artificial sweeteners is the concern about how our bodies are affected by artificial compounds over extended periods. Our bodily organs have evolved over thousands of years to process substances found in nature. The fact that our organs are capable of processing certain synthetic compounds without apparent ill effects does not mean that they can do so safely for long periods. Just as every drug has one or more undesirable side effects over time, it seems reasonable to assume that so too do all synthetic food compounds. Only time will tell which synthetics are the most dangerous. In the meantime, don't be one of the guinea pigs.

What You Can Do to Get the Sugar Out

- Become a food sleuth and start to examine food labels as if your life depended on it. Keep your total daily intake of sugars under 40 grams. If you have heart disease, cancer, obesity, blood sugar problems or any type of immune dysfunction, keep your daily intake below 20 grams.

- Avoid processed foods in general, especially those products that contain sugar or any word ending in "ose" in the list of ingredients.

- Choose sweets that have less than five grams of sugar per serving and preferably ones that contain blood-sugar balancing fiber, protein and fat to slow down the release of sugar (and the secretion of insulin) into your system.

- Satisfy your sweet tooth as much as possible the way nature intended—with natural, sugar-rich fruit and sweet vegetables such as squash and sweet potatoes. These sweet treats are loaded with fiber and nutrients, but you still should allow yourself no more than two to three servings of them per day.

- Eliminate refined white sugar from your diet. Use small amounts of natural sweeteners such as stevia, date sugar, maple syrup, rice syrup and fruit juice as transitions away from white sugar and toward a diet with very little concentrated sugar of any kind. In other words, gradually but consistently work at reducing the amount of sweeteners you use.

- Avoid using artificial sweeteners, which are associated with unpleasant side effects and health risks.

- Treat yourself to sweet experiences in place of sweet food. Sugar treats no longer seem so necessary when you allow yourself time for healthy indulgences.

- If you have blood sugar problems or sugar cravings, try using blood-sugar supporting nutrients. Here are seven of the most powerful sugar-fighting nutrients along with a suggested dosage for each for the most therapeutic benefit:

Nutrient	Daily Dosage
Chromium	200–600 mcg
B-complex vitamins	50 mg
L-Glutamine	500 mg three times a day
Manganese	10–30 mg
Pantothenic acid	500 mg
Vitamin C	3,000 mg
Zinc	30–50 mg

• Learn to beat the blood sugar blues by using the glycemic index, a classification of carbohydrates organized by their sugar/blood sugar/insulin interactions. The position of a food on the glycemic index (adapted from my book *Beyond Pritikin*) tells you whether it is recommended to eat plentifully, moderately or as little as possible. A food with a high position on the glycemic index is a rapid inducer of insulin and therefore is to be avoided or eaten only in small quantities.

Glycemic Index

High: 70% and up
Moderate: 40–69%
Low: 39% and below

The Glycemic Index of Carbohydrates

Rapid Inducers of Insulin

Greater than 100%

Corn flakes

40% bran flakes

French baguette

Instant white rice

Millet

Maltose

Puffed rice

Puffed wheat

Rice Krispies

Tofu ice cream substitute

Weetabix

100%

Glucose

White bread

Whole-wheat bread

90–99%

Apricots

Carrots

Corn chips

Grape-Nuts

Muesli

Parsnips

Shredded wheat

80–89%

Brown rice

Corn

Honey

Oat bran

Ripe banana

Ripe mango

Ripe papaya

Rolled oats

White potato

White rice

70–79%

All-Bran

Buckwheat

Kidney beans

Wheat (coarse)

Moderate Inducers of Insulin

60–69%

Apple juice
Applesauce
Beets
Bulgur
Couscous
Macaroni

Pinto beans
Pumpernickel bread
Raisins
Spaghetti (white or whole-wheat)
Wheat kernels

50–59%

Barley
Custard
Dried white beans
Green banana

Lactose
Peas (frozen)
Yam

40–49%

Bran
Butter beans
Grapes
Lima beans
Navy beans

Oatmeal (steel-cut)
Oranges
Peas (dried)
Rye (whole-grain)
Sweet potato

Reduced Insulin Secretion

30–39%

Apples
Black-eyed peas
Chickpeas
Milk (skim or whole)

Pears
Tomato soup
Yogurt

20–29%

Cherries	Peaches
Fructose	Plums
Grapefruit	
Lentils	

10–19%

Peanuts	Soybeans

All leafy green and other non-starchy vegetables plus eggs, fish, poultry and beef also have low glycemic index values.

4
Parasites:
Toxic Invader #2

Parasites are the second toxic invader that we must eliminate from our bodies. Now that we have removed sugar, the major food source of these uninvited guests, we are ready to eliminate the parasites themselves. Parasites are an unsuspected source of many baffling symptoms ranging from chronic fatigue and irritable bowel syndrome to overweight and even underweight as well as diarrhea and constipation. These creatures can zap our vitality and take our nutrients. They are a major health and beauty destroyer.

Unfortunately, many of us suffer—or know people who do—from mysterious maladies that affect our feeling of well-being and for which neither we nor our doctors can find a curable cause. Some treatments or medications help for a while, but the condition never entirely goes away. We frequently continue to have sensitivities, intolerances or allergies to various foods, often accompanied by depression. Our bodies tell us that something is physically wrong.

Most of us believe that parasites are a third-world problem. The reality is, however, that the United States is crawling with them. In the December 1990 issue of the *Townsend Letter for Doctors,* parasite expert Dr. Louis Parrish observed that at least eight out of ten of his patients showed signs of parasitic infection, either presently or in the past.

In my nutritional practice, I have seen many patients recover from undiagnosed illness after getting rid of parasites. Their ailments had been variously labeled depression, hypoglycemia, fatigue and environmental illness. As I took their history, I asked them what they liked to eat and which ethnic restaurants they frequented; I asked them where they had traveled and about their lifestyle in general. Their answers often so obviously pointed to parasitism that I had to assume their previous health care providers had not had this information. It was certainly not hard to see how previous recent travel, in particular, seemed to be associated with the onset of symptoms. A camping trip in the wilderness or a visit to South America, Asia or a tropical island frequently preceded persistent flulike symptoms, fatigue, allergy or gastrointestinal problems.

Illnesses caused or aggravated by parasites are not easy for doctors to diagnose, especially if the physician has no reason to suspect parasitism. The symptoms displayed are usually indicative of other disorders also, and the doctor is likely to select one of these. Additionally, many doctors neither know nor look for signs of parasites, which they have been educated in medical school to think of as "tropical medicine." Lack of watchfulness on the part of physicians is compounded by the inability of many lab technicians to detect the presence of specimens, larvae or eggs on a microscope slide, and by the complexity of some parasites' life cycles. All this explains why roundworm is mistaken for peptic ulcer, giardia for yeast infection, and tapeworm for hypoglycemia.

Although we are naturally repelled by the idea of creatures dwelling inside our bodies, we need to face up to this unwelcome possibility. Knowledge can protect us. When we know the dangers, we can much more easily avoid or neutralize them. With this in mind, grit your teeth and meet some nasty visitors.

Where Do Parasites Come From?

In my opinion, ten factors have combined over the past few decades to promote an epidemic of parasites in the United States. These factors include water contamination, imported or under-cooked foods, international travel, day-care centers, immigrants, armed forces overseas, pets, antibiotic and immunosuppressive drugs, sexual permissiveness and AIDS. Let's look briefly at each of these factors.

WATER CONTAMINATION

Cryptosporidium is now considered the leading cause of water-borne illness in America, according to the Environmental Protection Agency. In Milwaukee, during the spring of 1993, this tiny organism was the cause of 100 deaths and more than 400,000 cases of severe diarrhea and stomach problems. The organism was first identified in baby calves. Sewage leaks and agricultural run-off have permitted it to gain entrance to America's municipal water systems. In addition to Wisconsin, Texas, Georgia, Pennsylvania, Nevada and Oregon have reported cryptosporidium contamination.

Giardia is another parasitic contaminant of American fresh water. Dr. David Addiss at the Centers for Disease Control (CDC) in Atlanta points out that in the past 20 years the parasite has become plentiful in apparently unpolluted streams in the Rockies, Sierras, Northeast and Southeast. Unlike bacteria, neither giardia nor cryptosporidium is killed by chlorination.

IMPORTED OR UNDERCOOKED FOODS

In the spring of 1996, cyclospora-contaminated raspberries from Guatemala made national headlines when nearly 1,000 people who had eaten them developed diarrhea, severe gastrointestinal discomfort and fatigue. Since then, several other outbreaks have been reported involving raspberries imported from Guatemala and Chile.

Tapeworm infections have long been known to be caused by raw or undercooked meat, such as beef and pork. People normally cautious of domestic beef and pork, however, do not hesitate to consume a number of foreign dishes intended to be eaten raw, such as sushi, sashimi, steak tartare and pickled herring. These people are likely to find that tapeworms are as cosmopolitan as themselves.

Microwave cooking of fish can leave the interior less than thoroughly cooked. Besides tapeworm, some fish carry the larvae of anisakid worms, which in humans can cause anisakiasis, stomach ulcers and appendicitis. Fish known to be prone to carry anisakid larvae include Pacific salmon, rockfish (red snapper) and Atlantic haddock.

INTERNATIONAL TRAVEL

In 1990, more than 15 million Americans traveled abroad on business or for pleasure. Half of them visited underdeveloped countries. Giardia was perhaps the most frequent infection that they brought home, particularly those who had been to Russia, where the organisms can be found even in the tap water of some big cities.

The most dangerous parasite that Americans abroad are likely to be exposed to is the malaria organism. Almost two million deaths a year in a hundred countries are caused by malaria. Drug-resistant forms occur in South America, Southeast Asia and East Africa. Many geographic areas have their own special hazards, such as roundworms in China and the freshwater blood flukes that give schistosomiasis to bathers in Egypt.

DAY-CARE CENTERS

As we all know, very young children spread ailments to one another more frequently than adults do. The CDC estimated that 20,000 cases a year of giardia originated in day-care centers. An *In Health* magazine article by P.W. Moser cited a recent CDC survey in which the rate of giardia infection of all children in day-care centers was 25 percent in Fulton County, Georgia and 50 percent in New Haven, Connecticut. At a day-care center in Anaheim, California, the rate of giardia infection rose from 3 percent in 1981 to 43 percent in 1991.

Dennis Juranek, chief of CDC's Parasitic Disease Branch, thought that 20 percent of parents became infected themselves while tending their infected children.

IMMIGRANTS

Parasites thrive in unsanitary conditions in warm climates, and therefore many people who leave the tropics to work in other areas bring their parasite problems with them to their new home. Because many of these immigrants have few skills and a poor education, they find jobs at the lowest levels of the income scale. In American cities and suburbs, these jobs are often restaurant kitchen work or domestic or childcare work in homes. Their intimate contact with food and family provides any parasites they carry with a new world of opportunity.

ARMED FORCES OVERSEAS

Millions of Americans have served in parasite-infested Southeast Asia since the 1960s. More than a half million served in the Persian Gulf war. Discussion and lawsuits continue today over what illnesses members of the armed forces contracted while on overseas duty. The only thing beyond disagreement is that illness caused far more casualties than combat.

Those who became sick while still in the armed forces were more likely to have their parasitic illnesses recognized for what they were than those who developed symptoms after they left the armed forces. In any event, many brought home parasites undetected either by medical authorities or themselves.

PETS

Of the 240 infectious diseases that humans catch from animals, 65 are transmitted by dogs and 39 by cats. Americans keep some 110 million dogs and cats as pets, with nearly 90 percent of the cats sleeping on human beds. The parasites dogs and cats transmit to humans almost always go unsuspected and unrecognized. These parasites include roundworm, hookworm and the toxoplasmosis organism.

Antibiotic and Immunosuppressive Drugs

A healthy person's immune system can fight bacteria and viruses successfully. We don't have much medical knowledge of a healthy body's natural defenses against parasites, but we do know that people who are rundown or have a suppressed immune system are more vulnerable to parasites than are healthy people. Taking antibiotics for an infection can cause beneficial bacteria in the vagina and intestines to be destroyed as well as the harmful bacteria, resulting in yeast overgrowth or trichomoniasis. Taking immunosuppressive drugs increases the risk of toxoplasmosis.

Sexual Permissiveness

An increased number of sex partners increases the chances of sexually transmitted parasitism. When two sexual partners each have their own multiple sexual partners, and when many of these sexual partners in turn have multiple sexual partners, the possibilities of venereal parasitic infection multiply alarmingly.

AIDS

Researchers have found evidence that infection by amoebic parasites seems to make people more vulnerable to later infection by the AIDS virus. This may be caused by amoebic damage to immune system cells that attack the AIDS virus. People who are already HIV-positive become vulnerable to a whole array of opportunistic parasites, in particular the organisms for pneumocystic pneumonia, cryptosporidiosis, and strongyloidiasis.

How Parasites Invade the Body

At some time during their lives, one in two Americans becomes a host to endoparasites. Endoparasites occur within the body, as distinct from ectoparasites, such as fleas or ticks, which dwell on the skin or in the hair.

The following are the four major pathways by which parasites invade human beings:

- **Infected water and food.** Giardia, amoeba and roundworm are typically transmitted in this way.
- **Vector.** A vector is a nonhuman that transmits the parasite and that may or may not be infected itself. For example, mosquitoes transmit the malaria parasite, houseflies transmit amoebic cysts, and sandflies transmit the leishmaniasis parasite.
- **Sexual contact.** Giardia, amoeba, and trichomonas are among the parasites frequently passed from one sexual partner to another.
- **Skin and respiratory tract.** Unlike the mouth and gastrointestinal tract, the nose and respiratory tract are unprotected by acidic secretions. Dust breathed in can be infected with pinworm eggs and *Toxoplasma gondii*. The pores of the skin and cuts are also entrance ways for microscopic organisms. Schistosomes, hookworms and strongyloides can enter the body through the skin.

Symptoms of Parasitism

Practically any part of our body can be affected by parasites. Even the eyes, brain and heart are vulnerable. But the greatest number of kinds of parasites live in the small intestine, with the colon and then the blood and lymph systems as the other most likely dwelling places. In their often complex life cycles, which can involve one or more very dissimilar egg, larva, adult and cyst stages, parasites may invade the lungs or tunnel into muscle or other tissue.

Most parasites in the body sooner or later make their presence known through physical discomfort. But most of these symptoms are not characteristic of parasites only—they could also be caused by nonparasitic ailments. Indeed, more often than not, they are diagnosed as such by doctors who do not consider or too readily dismiss the possibility of parasites.

The following are the major symptoms of parasitic infection. When people suffer from one or more of these symptoms over time without adequate medical explanation, the possibility of parasites needs at least to be seriously considered.

- **Constipation.** Worms, either because of their large size or great number, can obstruct passage through the intestines.

- **Diarrhea.** Some parasites, mostly protozoans, secrete a hormonelike substance that causes a sodium and chloride loss, resulting in frequent watery stool.

- **Gas and bloating.** Parasites in the upper small intestine can cause inflammation that results in gas and bloating, particularly when raw fruit, raw vegetables, beans or other hard-to-digest foods are eaten.

- **Irritable bowel syndrome.** By irritating, inflaming and coating intestinal walls, parasites can interfere with food absorption, causing bulky stools and excess fat in the feces.

- **Joint and muscle discomfort.** Parasites can encyst in joint fluids or muscle tissue. The discomfort this causes may be diagnosed as arthritis.

- **Anemia.** Some worms attach themselves to the intestinal lining and take nutrients from the blood of their human host. Large numbers of them can cause pernicious anemia or an iron deficiency.

- **Allergy.** By irritating and sometimes even perforating the intestinal lining, parasites can cause large undigested molecules to enter and activate an immune response. The immune response can end in an allergic reaction.

- **Skin conditions.** Protozoan parasites can cause swellings, sores, papular lesions, dermatitis and skin ulcers. Intestinal worms can be responsible for rashes, eczema, hives and other allergylike skin conditions.

- **Granulomas.** These knots of tissue form around dead parasite larvae or eggs. Most often found in the colon and rectal walls, they also occur in the liver, lungs, uterus and peritoneum.

- **Nervousness.** Excretion and toxic waste of parasites can irritate the human nervous system, resulting in restlessness and anxiety.

- **Sleep disturbances.** Some parasites can cause discomfort when they exit through the anus, waking their host. Practitioners of Chinese medicine claim that the early morning hour of 2 to 3 A.M. is governed by the liver, and that wakefulness may result at this time as the liver processes toxic products from parasites.

- **Teeth grinding.** This has been observed, particularly in sleeping children, in cases of parasitism. The teeth grinding may be a nervous response to an internal irritant.

- **Chronic fatigue.** Malnutrition caused by parasites can cause the fatigue, depression and other symptoms characteristic of this syndrome.

- **Immune dysfunction.** By continually stimulating immune responses by their presence, parasites can wear down the immune system and make it less responsive to other threats.

Kinds of Parasites

According to one dictionary definition of a parasite, it is someone who frequents the tables of the rich and who earns a welcome through flattery. But in reality, most parasites skip the flattery and are very democratic about their potential host's economic status. The term *parasite,* however, is not a scientific one, with a concise meaning. My use of the term refers to an organism living in the body, an internal hitchhiker if you will, that is sapping the energy of its host and absorbing its life force in a harmful way.

Parasites are divided into five categories:

- One-celled organisms (protozoans)
- Roundworms, pinworms, hookworms (nematodes)
- Tapeworms (cestodes)
- Flukes (trematodes)
- Tick-borne organisms

In the following sections, we will briefly meet some of the more prominent members of each category that are currently being diagnosed in the United States.

PROTOZOANS

Although most of these one-celled organisms are so small they are invisible to the naked eye, the trouble they cause is all out of proportion to their size. Some breed rapidly and cause problems through their power of numbers. Some can encyst, that is, enter a hard-walled stage, that can survive in a hostile environment after being expelled from one body and before being ingested by another.

Blastocystis hominis. Once thought to be a yeast, this organism is now regarded as a protozoan but with many similarities to a plant fungus. It was once thought to be harmless but is now known to cause gastrointestinal symptoms such as diarrhea, nausea and abdominal cramps and pain. In a 1996 study of 44 people infected by this organism, 18 had been to India, Nepal or Pakistan. Even after two years of treatment, some had not managed to rid themselves of the protozoan.

Cryptosporidium muris. This organism is transmitted by groundwater, domestic animals, and the fecal-oral route, especially through diaper changing and in day-care centers. Otherwise healthy people have mild symptoms of nausea, fever, abdominal discomfort, diarrhea or weight loss. The condition can be fatal in people with compromised immune systems. As previously stated, *Cryptosporidium* in the city's water supply was responsible for more than 400,000 people becoming ill in Milwaukee in 1993, resulting in 100 deaths.

No treatment is known for this condition, and prevention is the only practical approach at present. A healthy, strong immune system helps people fight this organism. Children under the age of two, whose immune systems are not fully developed, are vulnerable, as are people with a compromised immune system, particularly those with AIDS.

Cyclospora cayetanensis. The first reported *Cyclospora* outbreak in America took place in 1994. Only two years later, almost 1,000 Americans were made ill by contaminated raspberries imported from Guatemala. This outbreak, in the spring of 1996, was the first time it was proved beyond doubt that parasites could travel in food and cause infection at its destination. A CDC epidemiologist observed, however, that a native population of *Cyclospora* exists in the United States, although it was not involved in this outbreak. Gastric symptoms included diarrhea, bloating, flatulence, cramps, constipation, vomiting and poor absorption of nutrients. Other symptoms included anemia, headache, fatigue, nausea, depression, muscle aches and weakness. Treatment with antibiotics is effective.

Entamoeba histolytica. Humans are infected by this amoeba in cyst form. The cysts may be in food or water contaminated by an infected person, flies or cockroaches. After the cyst is swallowed, it becomes a free-swimming trophozoite in the small intestine, where it multiplies. The symptoms are often so mild that people don't know they are infected. Abdominal distention, fever, dysentery, hepatitis or liver, lung or brain abscesses can be more serious consequences. The trophozoite can also penetrate the intestinal lining and invade the liver, lungs, heart and brain.

Giardia lamblia. This organism's cysts are transmitted in contaminated food, water or animal feces. City tap water, clear mountain streams and well water are frequently the source of infection, as are the droppings of pet dogs, cats and parakeets. Infection often occurs at day-care centers and during anal-oral sex. The cyst becomes a trophozoite and uses a sucking disk to adhere to the upper intestine wall. Symptoms of infection include diarrhea, nausea, bloating, abdominal cramps, weight loss and oily stool. Long-term infection can produce nutritional deficiencies, lactose intolerance, celiac/sprue and depression.

ROUNDWORMS, PINWORMS, HOOKWORMS (NEMATODES)

Nematode parasitic worms often exist unnoticed by their human hosts. Symptoms tend to first appear when the infection becomes heavy.

Roundworm. The ascaris roundworm (*Ascaris lumbricoides*) is the most common intestinal parasite throughout the world, with perhaps a total of a billion infected people. Humans become infected by roundworm eggs in soil or food. The worm lives in the intestines, but can travel through the body to the heart, liver and lungs. Symptoms vary and tend to be more severe in children.

Hookworm. The larvae of two hookworm species (*Necator americanus* and *Ancylostoma duodenal*) live in warm, moist soil and can penetrate human skin, often that of barefoot people. The larvae pass through the bloodstream into the lungs; from there into the respiratory tract and throat; and then down into the small intestine—a journey that takes about seven weeks. Once in the small intestine, individual hookworms can live for up to 15 years. Found worldwide in moist, warm climates, hookworms are most prevalent in the southeastern United States. Itchy skin and pimples or blisters known as ground or dew itch are early symptoms of infection. Pneumonia, bronchitis, anemia, weight loss, anorexia, nausea or dizziness may be later symptoms.

Pinworm. This is the most frequently found American parasitic worm, particularly in children. Humans pass it on to one another, and it can also be picked up from contaminated food, water or house dust. The female pinworm moves outside the host's anus in order to lay eggs, often creating itchiness. Children, after their fingers have scratched the itch, can pass on eggs to other children or adults or to food, or they can reinfect themselves through the mouth. Sheets, toilet seats, and bathtubs can also be sites of infection. Itching is a characteristic symptom. My childhood pediatrician, Leo Litter from West Hartford, Connecticut, has documented far more serious problems associated with infestations, including vision problems, epilepsy, abnormal EEGs and hyperactivity.

Tapeworms (Cestodes)

Tapeworms are flat and ribbonlike, consisting of a head that attaches to the intestinal wall and a number of segments. Beef, pork and fish tapeworms are all transmitted by raw or undercooked meat.

Beef Tapeworm. Usually occurring singly and causing few symptoms, this tapeworm often makes its presence known by segments exiting from the anus.

Pork Tapeworm. Usually occurring in a multiple infection, this tapeworm is the most dangerous to humans because its larvae burrow into muscle tissue and can spread along the central nervous system into other tissues and organs, including the brain, heart and eyes.

Fish Tapeworm. The largest human parasite, it is found in some freshwater and migratory fish, including perch, pike, pickerel, Alaskan salmon and American turbot in the Great Lakes, Canada and Alaska as well as Japan, Australia, Russia and Scandinavia. Abdominal pain, nausea and anorexia are frequent symptoms. This tapeworm can cause a vitamin B-12 deficiency by consuming most of this vitamin in the host's food.

Dog Tapeworm. Children kissing dogs may accidentally swallow infected dog fleas and develop pumpkin seed tapeworm, so called because its segments resemble pumpkin seeds in a child's stool or undergarments. Its symptoms include diarrhea and restlessness.

FLUKES (TREMATODES)

The stage infective to humans in the life cycle of these leaf-shaped flatworms is a larval one. The free-swimming larvae are released into freshwater by infected snails. Although flukes are not a threat in North America, they can be picked up by travelers in many parts of the world. They include the following: liver fluke from undercooked fish (in Hawaii), sheep liver fluke from water-cress, Oriental lung fluke from undercooked crabs and crayfish and intestinal fluke from the unpeeled skin of water chestnuts, bamboo shoots, lotus roots and other plants.

TICK-BORNE ORGANISMS

Besides Lyme disease, eight other less common tick-borne diseases occur in North America. As we learn more about these disorders, it is becoming evident that some of them are more prevalent than previously believed.

Lyme Disease. This disorder is caused by the spirochete bacterium *Borrelia burgdorferi,* of which there are more than 100 different strains in America. A number of ticks can transmit this bacterium to humans. By far the most frequent vectors in America are the black-legged tick (*Ixodes scapularis*) and the Western black-legged tick (*I. pacificus*). An individual tick may carry several strains of the infectious agent.

The severity of the illness varies widely, as do the kinds of symptoms. Early diagnosis allows early treatment and often complete recovery with only minor symptoms. But the symptoms at any stage are easy for a doctor to misdiagnose. When the disease becomes entrenched in the body, it may be very difficult to eradicate.

The CDC has reported 81,000 confirmed cases of Lyme disease since 1982. Some researchers and clinicians believe, however, that this may amount to only 10 percent of the number of actual cases. A 1996 Connecticut Department of Public Health Survey found that only 1 in 13 cases was being reported. If this disparity between real and reported cases exists, more than a million cases of Lyme disease may have occurred in America in the past 15 years.

The Lyme disease pathogen enters the human bloodstream through a tick bite in the skin. The pathogen is intracellular, meaning that it lives inside cells, which can help it evade medical detection. It can invade the cells of the immune system.

Other tick-borne diseases include Rocky Mountain spotted fever, ehrlichiosis, Colorado tick fever, babesiosis, relapsing fever, tularemia, Powassan encephalitis and tick paralysis.

Cutting-edge Parasite Testing

In May 1997, ABC World News Tonight reported a major technological breakthrough in parasite testing. Utilizing special computers to dissect the DNA of parasites, Stanford University School of Medicine researchers genetically analyzed various parasite species. It may be only a matter of time before scientists can duplicate this breakthrough in genetic technology on a computer chip for use all over the country.

What You Can Do to Rid Yourself of Parasites

Intestinal cleansing. There are many intestinal cleansing products available in the health food store that will start the process of flushing out parasites and their protective mucus layers from the intestines. Parasites clinging to the intestinal lining may be protected by an overlying layer of mucus or encrusted waste matter. As bulking agents move through the intestines, they take toxins and accumulated waste matter with them, removing protective layers from the parasite that are not swept out along with them.

There are many fine intestinal cleansing products on the market. My clients and readers have reported remarkable elimination using the Uni Key Elimination Formula (see Resources).

Colonic irrigations. A series of colonic irrigations, also known as high colonics or high enemas, can also assist the cleansing process. A colonic involves irrigating the entire length of the colon or large intestine with a lukewarm water solution. The solution dislodges and removes toxins from hard-to-reach pockets where fecal matter has a tendency to accumulate. The procedure takes about three-quarters of an hour and is usually conducted in a health professional's office by a certified colon hydrotherapist. Make sure your colon therapist uses water that has been filtered to remove chemicals, heavy metals and parasites. Also, make sure that additional antiseptic measures, such as the use of disposable tubing, are part of the procedure.

My colonic therapist, Sherri Boylan in Belgrade, Montana, believes that a colonic can eliminate volumes of impacted fecal material and excess mucus as well as harmful bacteria, parasites and worms. She states that a colonic can also help to reestablish the original shape of the colon. Bulges and pockets where waste material may have been hiding are reformed back into their normal shape. A colonic exercises and tones the muscles of the colon, teaching them to once again initiate peristaltic action to move waste material out. Finally, Sherri believes that colon hydrotherapy can reestablish the habit of regular bowel movements. It can rid the body of constipation and diarrhea and help it eliminate regularly. Once the system has been cleaned with colon hydrotherapy, the colon can again function as it was meant to, eliminating unwanted wastes from the body.

Enemas can be easily done at home. However, enemas reach only the lower 12½ inches of the colon, whereas colonic irrigation cleanses its entire length of 5½ feet. Adding garlic juice to an enema increases its antiparasitic powers. An enema made from two mashed garlic cloves boiled (then cooled) in six ounces of milk given for three consecutive nights will kill pinworms in children. Vinegar enemas are an effective general detoxifier. Add two tablespoons of apple cider vinegar to one quart of water. Blackstrap molasses enemas can pull encrusted fecal matter and parasites off the colon lining and seem to relax the colon. Add one tablespoon of molasses to a quart of water. Coffee enemas will be discussed in Chapter 12.

In preparing an enema, only filtered water or distilled water boiled for at least ten minutes should be used. The enema bag and tubing should be sterilized after each use by soaking them for 15 minutes in a diluted Clorox bath (a half-teaspoon of Clorox to a gallon of water).

Parasite removal. After a month of weekly intestinal cleansing, you are ready to remove the parasites themselves at all stages of their development. Over the past 20 years, I have found that certain herbal formulations are very unfriendly to parasites. The most successful that I personally use and recommend are four products made by Uni Key Health Systems (see Resources). They include Verma-Key, Verma-Plus, Para-Key and Para-Plus. For general parasite removal, when you don't know exactly what you may be carrying, I recommend the Verma program first, followed by the Para program. Verma-Key is for worms and flukes. The capsules contain black walnut, wormwood, balmony, wormseed, the laxative cascara sagrada, slippery elm, garlic and cloves. Verma-Plus, a liquid herbal tincture, is also for worms and flukes. It contains black walnut, wormwood, centaury, male fern, orange peel, cloves and butternut in a base of 20 percent alcohol and water. The Verma products should be used simultaneously for two months.

The two Para products for protozoans are Para-Key capsules, which contain cranberry concentrate, grapefruit seed extract, artemisia annua, garlic, cayenne, slippery elm and bromelain and the liquid herbal tincture Para-Plus, which contains black walnut, artemisia annua, prickly ash bark, quassia bark, cloves and cranberry concentrate in a base of 20 percent alcohol and water. The Para products should also be used simultaneously for two months.

After the parasites appear to be cleared from a person's system, I usually recommend Zymex II to mop up any eggs or larvae that may persist in the intestines. These capsules, made by Standard Process Labs and available through health practitioners or Uni Key (see Resources), consist of a combination of proteolytic enzymes from almond flour, fig powder, papain and bromelain along with lipase, cellulase and amylase.

Drugs. Of course, there are many prescription and over-the-counter drugs for parasites. If your doctor recommends one, check out its side effects before using it. For example, the drug Flagyl (metronidazole), widely used for giardasis, amebiasis and trichomoniasis, can cause a metallic taste, headache, nausea and disorientation. Worse still, it can encourage yeast growth. And to add insult to injury, many protozoans seem to have developed a resistance to it.

Introducing friendly bacteria. After both the intestinal and parasite cleansing, you are ready to recolonize the intestines with friendly bacteria, since heavy-duty cleansing will have killed off many of the previous residents, and their niches may now be occupied by less beneficial bacteria. This is now your number-one priority. To recover a normal, healthy digestive system, most people need at least one, and perhaps all four, of the following friendly intestinal bacteria: *Lactobacillus acidophilus, L. bulgaris, L. bifidus* and *Streptococcus faeceum.* I personally use Uni Key Flora Balance.

Friendly intestinal bacteria are available in liquid, powder and pill form in health food stores. You need to read the labels carefully and follow the instructions exactly. In this case, more may not be better. Daily use helps rebuild a strong digestive system.

When choosing a digestive aid, avoid those containing bile or bile salts, because parasites (especially giardia) feed on them.

People with intestinal parasites face a paradox. The more they build up their resistance through nutrition and dietary supplements like antioxidants, iron and vitamin B-12, the more they feed their parasites. Yet by starving their parasites, they risk lowering their own resistance to them.

Diet. My clinical practice of many years has shown me that there actually is a diet that favors the host over the parasite. In its most popular form, it is known as the 40/30/30 diet. In it, 40 percent of calories come from carbohydrates, 30 percent from fats and 30 percent from protein. Why does this diet discourage parasites? First of all, because high protein intake makes parasites weaken their hold on intestinal walls. And, second, because this diet almost totally excludes sugar. Lots of sugar dissolved in water makes the intestine a vacation resort for parasites. They can eat to their hearts' content without ever having to work for a meal. Depriving parasites of free and easy nutrition makes it harder for them to thrive. Meanwhile, their host grows stronger on a healthy diet.

In addition to the 40/30/30 diet plan, you can weaken parasites by eating certain foods they find disagreeable. The following foods are all worth including in your diet because parasites don't like them at all:

Almonds, ground	Papaya juice
Blackberries	Papaya seeds
Cabbage, raw	Pineapple juice
Carrot greens	Pomegranate juice
Fig extract	Pumpkin
Garlic cloves	Pumpkin seeds, finely ground
Kelp	Radish roots
Onions	Sauerkraut

Testing for Parasites. If you would like to find out definitively which internal hitchhikers you may be carrying, you should get tested. You can call Uni Key Health Systems (see Resources) to order a state-of-the-art purged stool test kit that has been made available to my readers and clients through an association between my office, Uni Key, and a certified parasite laboratory. The stool sample, collected in the privacy of your home, is sent directly to one of the top parasitology labs and is examined for more than a dozen protozoans, 15 types of worms and the common yeasts (including *Candida albicans*) and fungi spores. Results are sent to my office, where a personalized recommendation is made. The recommendation may include natural products, nutritional supplements and diet, should you choose the natural route. The kit contains a saline laxative, a collection basin and mailing containers, plus complete step-by-step instructions for collecting the sample.

9 Ways to Avoid Parasites

1. Boil tap water for at least 20 minutes or consider buying a home filter that removes organisms as small as .05 microns from drinking water and that has been certified to block parasitic cysts. I personally use the Doulton water filter throughout my home and office (see Resources).
2. Avoid salad bars.
3. Don't eat imported fruit (especially raspberries) or raw, rare or undercooked pork, other meat or fish.
4. Use a brush to scrub under your fingernails where cysts can hide out.
5. When eating out in questionable restaurants here or abroad, select well-cooked food and peeled fruits and vegetables.
6. For both traveling and camping, use a portable water filter.
7. After handling your pet, wash your hands.
8. Use onions, garlic, cloves or fennel in cooking.
9. Get the sugar out!

LYME DISEASE PREVENTION

A painless bite from a deer tick the size of a pinhead can cause fever, headache, a stiff neck, fatigue, listlessness and a red bullseye on the skin around the bite. If treatment is not received because these symptoms do not appear or are ignored, more serious symptoms like arthritis, meningitis, Bell's palsy, severe pain, numbness, tingling and burning feelings at the extremities, depression or fatigue may appear later. Heart, eye, respiratory and gastrointestinal problems are also possible. It's clearly worth avoiding a bite by an infected deer tick. Here are the simple precautions that you need to take.

- Don't go into moist, wooded places that are likely to be infested with ticks.
- If you must go into such places, keep away from vegetation and don't sit on the ground.
- Before going into suspect areas, apply an EPA-approved tick repellent to your skin and clothes.
- Wear a light-colored, long-sleeved blouse or shirt and light-colored pants tucked into your socks. The tiny dark ticks are easier to see against a light background.
- Wash and dry your clothes as soon as you get back.

If you think you have been bitten, see a doctor. The most effective treatment is deoxycycline, an oral antibiotic sold under several brand names. Another effective treatment is ceftriaxone (brand name Rocephin), an antibiotic given by injection.

5

Heavy Metals:
Toxic Invader #3

Getting rid of sugar and parasites is in some ways easier than freeing ourselves of heavy metals. Aluminum, lead, mercury and copper are so pervasive in 20th-century life that it is almost impossible to figure out which metal is to blame for one's ill health. Most readers are aware of some of the health hazards from aluminum (antacids, cookware, antiperspirants), lead (industrial waste), mercury (dental fillings) and copper (water pipes). But this is only the beginning. Evidence is now emerging that suggests that many of these and other metals suppress the immune system by producing free radicals, which in turn help to accelerate the aging process as well as degenerative disease.

The metals discussed in this chapter are all in everyday use. While some are actually therapeutic and beneficial in small amounts (copper, iron and manganese, for example), they can be toxic in greater quantities. Others, like mercury, aluminum and lead, can be toxic to certain individuals no matter how small the amount.

Certain categories of people are prone to overexposure to some or all of these metals, such as individuals who work in the mining, smelting or refining industries. Hobbyists, especially those who spend a lot of time doing fine detail at close quarters, as well as potters, painters and sculptors, are also at risk as are children who get their hands on adult art supplies or mineral supplements (particularly those containing iron).

I consider the removal and avoidance of toxic metals to be an essential part of the antiaging program. My mentor, Dr. Hazel Parcells, always said that the best way to ensure life extension and youth was through the elimination of parasites, heavy metals and radiation—in that order. After discussing the toxic metal sources all around us, I will tell you how to eliminate their toxic effects.

Aluminum

In daily life, we are most likely to ingest excess aluminum from antacids (Maalox, Mylanta and Gelusil), pain relievers (Bufferin, Arthritis-strength Bufferin, Vanquish), pickles, antiperspirants, cosmetics and the ubiquitous aluminum pots and pans. As Dr. Parcells once warned in a class she taught in the mid-1970s in Albuquerque, New Mexico, "I'd rather have the most deadly serpent in the kitchen than a single aluminum pot or pan." She was also deadset against aluminum foil for cooking or even for covering foods.

This made such a lasting impression on me that when I returned to my home in Connecticut I threw out every aluminum utensil I owned—tea kettles, strainers, measuring cups, measuring spoons, pots and pans. I also disposed of my mother's aluminum cookware. Although she may not have appreciated it then, based upon all the research we have today that links aluminum with Alzheimer's, ulcers, heart disease and other health conditions, I believe she is thankful today.

Some researchers contend that fluoride in the water increases the leaching of aluminum from aluminum pots and pans. Metalworkers, jewelers and potters often exceed permissible exposure limits.

Symptoms such as dryness of the skin and mucous membranes,

heartburn, colic, headaches, flatulence and a tendency to frequently come down with colds may be associated with early signs of aluminum toxicity. Long-term symptoms can include memory loss, mental confusion, Parkinson's disease and amyotrophic lateral sclerosis.

Aluminum has also been found to compromise digestion because it has a tendency to neutralize the protein-digestive enzyme pepsin in the stomach. In addition, it interferes with the body's ability to use magnesium, calcium and phosphorus, putting one at risk for osteoporosis. Impaired motor coordination as well as Alzheimer's disease have both been associated with exposure to aluminum. As Michael A. Weiner, Ph.D. has written, "Autopsies of people who have died with Alzheimer's reveal aluminum in the distinctive nerve cell plaques in the cerebral cortex. . . . Here's how to decrease your aluminum level now: Get rid of all aluminum pots and pans, including those with aluminum sandwiched between steel." The brain, kidneys and GI tract are the major areas where aluminum accumulates and causes harm.

Antimony

Antimony is found in dental materials, dyes, pigments, lacquers, glazes, enamels, pottery, glass, abrasives, flame-proofing substances, drugs for tropical diseases, battery components, ant poison, explosives, fireworks and matches. Glassblowers, potters, painters, dyers and solderers are likely to exceed permissible limits of exposure to this metal. Antimony is associated with lung cancer, miscarriage and premature birth, disruption of the menstrual cycle and accidental poisoning of children. We can inhale antimony in fumes, ingest it or absorb it through our skin.

Inhalation symptoms include a flulike fever plus a metallic

taste in the mouth; coughing; breathing difficulties; irritation of eyes, ears, nose and throat; headache; nausea; vomiting; muscular pain and fatigue. Swallowing antimony causes mouth, nose and stomach irritation, nausea, vomiting, breathing difficulties, coma and death. Acids reacting with antimony cause the release of a very toxic gas called stibine.

Arsenic

The toxic metal arsenic may be somewhat more familiar because of its role in the classic mystery *Arsenic and Old Lace*. In reality, arsenic is easy to detect and would not be very effective as a poison, the purpose intended in Joseph Kesselring's well-loved play. Arsenic, does, however, make people feel very ill and can also affect fertility by causing chromosome damage.

Smoke from a stove burning arsenic-treated wood, tobacco smoke, polluted air and water, coal dust, weed killers, insecticides, rodenticides, fungicides and some paints contain arsenic. Whiskey from illicit stills may contain it, and street drugs like heroin and cocaine may be diluted with it. Children are poisoned by getting arsenic-containing antipest compounds on their fingers and then putting their fingers in their mouths.

Breathing in arsenic or dust causes coughing, difficulty in breathing, restlessness and the blue-gray skin discoloration known as cyanosis. Ingestion of arsenic over a long period causes characteristic horizontal white bands or longitudinal brown bands on the nails, brown discoloration of nails, loss of nails, skin discoloration, nausea, vomiting and diarrhea. Additionally, numbness of limbs, visual impairment and deafness can occur, as well as memory loss, changes in thought patterns and loss of coordination.

Cadmium

We are most likely to be exposed to cadmium from cigarette smoking or second-hand smoke because cadmium is the most prominent metal in cured tobacco. Other common sources include metal containers of food or drink. Cookware with a cadmium-containing glaze, electroplated ice-cube trays and cadmium-containing solders in vending machines that dispense liquids are frequent sources of the metal. Other sources include pesticides, antiseptics and medications for dandruff and oily skin. Jewelers, potters, welders, painters, sculptors and photographers are subject to still other dangers of heavy exposure. Children with access to adult art pigments may accidentally poison themselves.

Cadmium has been linked to lung and prostate cancer, chromosome damage and reduced birth weight. Loss of smell, runny nose, shortness of breath, coughing, weight loss, irritability and fatigue result from long-term exposure to cadmium fumes, accompanied by yellow rings on the teeth, bone pain and kidney damage.

Copper

Before reviewing the prevalence of copper toxicity in 20th-century society, let's review some historical connections to heavy metal poisonings. Many well-respected historians believe that the Romans were the first society to be destroyed by heavy metal poisoning. Lead was the heavy metal culprit of the ancient Romans, and it led to mental retardation as well as infertility among the Roman upper classes. According to noted researcher Dr. Jerome O. Nriagu, the consumption of wine alone may have contributed to the heavy doses of lead to which the Romans were exposed. The Romans flavored their wine by simmering the grape juice in lead pots or lead-lined copper kettles. The acidic nature of the grapes extracted large amounts of lead from the utensils. Lead has a very sweet taste and so enhanced the natural sweetness of the wine. Thus lead has earned the reputation as the "sweet poison."

What does this have to do with copper and our modern day society? According to the cutting-edge research of Dr. Paul C. Eck of Analytical Research Laboratories in Phoenix, Arizona, copper is to America today what lead was to the ancient Romans, because both were unsuspected toxins in their respective societies. Today, copper may very well be a fundamental cause of debilitating and aging biochemical imbalances.

Eck believes that copper toxicity can occur because of environmental exposure, dietary excess and endocrine imbalance. The environmental copper sources include copper plumbing, copper cookware, naturally occurring copper in water, birth control pills, copper intrauterine devices, dental amalgams and fungicides for swimming pools and foods. Those whose hair analyses show copper overload should eat only limited amounts of copper-rich foods. These include soy (in tempeh, tofu and soy protein powders), nuts, seeds, avocadoes and grains; shellfish such as oysters, lobster, crab and shrimp; chocolate, regular tea, wheat germ, bran and brewer's yeast.

Adrenal gland exhaustion also contributes to copper toxicity because of a series of biochemical adaptive processes which depresses the production of the copper-binding protein, ceruloplasmin, in the liver. This ultimately results in the accumulation of excess or biounavailable copper in various tissues and organs.

Common symptoms which are associated with copper toxicity include depression, insomnia, anorexia nervosa, compulsive behavior, anxiety, hyperactivity, various skin disorders, hair loss and allergies. Eck suggests that "copperhead" personality types are distinguished by their highly charged nervous systems, which cause compulsive and sometimes addictive behaviors. These individuals are highly creative and intensely hyperactive.

Many years ago I worked with a nutritionally oriented psychiatrist at Deepbrook Associates in Newtown, Connecticut who systematically took hair samples from every new patient. Unbelievably, he would find that many of the children he was treating who were suffering from learning disabilities and hyperactivity were suffering from a copper imbalance. Once the copper was in check, the hyperactive symptoms disappeared.

Many female disorders such as PMS, endometriosis, fibroid tumors and other menstrual irregularities may be linked to excess tissue copper. Likewise, many male disorders, such as sexual impotence, overaggressiveness and hair loss can be attributed to copper toxicity.

There are a number of metabolic functions which are dependent upon balanced copper metabolism. These include the formation of the myelin nerve sheaths, synthesis of neurotransmitters, formation of keratin and melanin, fertility and the synthesis of the body's connective tissue. For more information on copper overload, please refer to my book *Why Am I Always So Tired?* (Harper San Francisco, 1999).

Iron

In just the right biochemical amounts, iron is a carrier of oxygen throughout the body and helps to contribute to strong blood and a well-functioning circulatory system, preventing cold hands, fatigue, lusterless hair and pale skin. In excess, however, iron is a potent free radical instigator and can dramatically increase the risk of heart disease and cancer. We are exposed to iron in a number of seemingly tame dietary sources. It is added to white flour during the enrichment process and so is contained in most baked goods like breads, cereals, crackers, pasta, cakes and cookies. It is naturally available in red meat. It is also a prominent mineral that is added to many over-the-counter vitamin/mineral preparations. Its absorption is markedly enhanced in the system with vitamin C supplementation, and we all know how popular vitamin C has become these days.

As many as 1 in 300 Americans suffer from a genetic condition known as hemachromatosis in which the body stores iron in its tissues and organs. The symptoms of iron overload mirror those of iron deficiency, anemia being one of the key symptoms. Fatigue, low immunity, abdominal pain, lack of mental clarity and a grayish/bronze tint to the skin (the look of a perpetual suntan) are also characteristic of this condition.

Over time, iron overload can cause organ failure, resulting in conditions like arthritis, diabetes, impotence, sterility, premature menopause and cirrhosis.

Lead

Government statistics show that in 1994 almost 1.7 million young children had excessively high blood levels of lead. This amounts to almost 9 percent of all preschool children in the United States. In 1991, the CDC called lead poisoning "the most common and socially devastating environmental disease of young children." In addition to its physical effects, lead poisoning damages children's brains. Even in small amounts, lead slows young children's mental development, lowers their intelligence level and is responsible for learning disabilities and behavioral problems. Attention deficit disorder and hyperactivity have been linked to lead exposure. How lead causes these problems is not known.

The bodies of young children absorb more lead than adults. Lead-containing paint is thought to be the chief cause of lead poisoning in young children in rundown urban neighborhoods. Chips of paint inadvertently or deliberately swallowed (remember, lead tastes sweet) and dust breathed in from houses under renovation are probably the most frequent sources. Lead also leaches into water from lead pipes, and into food and drinks from some pottery. Further sources of lead include toys, contaminated food and water and polluted air and soil. Nursing mothers with high blood levels of lead have contaminated breast milk.

In October 1997, the Greenpeace organization reported that a wide variety of plastic household items contain dangerously high levels of lead. These include toys, raincoats and telephone cords. According to the report, when subjected to heat and sunlight, the plastic breaks down and the toxic lead becomes available. The Consumer Products Safety Commission responded that a quick check of some of the products mentioned in the report revealed no problems, but acknowledged that the products had not been subjected to heat or sunlight.

With the adoption of lead-free gasoline in the United States, adult blood levels of lead declined. Today adult exposure to lead most often occurs in the workplace, and through the residues on work clothes and shoes brought into the home. Antique china can also dish out lead. Sniffing gasoline causes insomnia, disturbing dreams, nausea, vomiting, restlessness, anxiety and irritability. Longer-term exposure leads to tremors, twitching of face muscles, jerking of limbs, confusion, mania and seizures. Lead poisoning can lead to damaged vision, a characteristic blue gumline, hearing loss, gastric pain, menstrual irregularities, kidney disease, miscarriage, convulsions, coma and death.

Manganese

Manganese, like iron, can function as a double-edged sword. It is essential for the formation of certain enzymes, helps the reproductive system, assists in blood sugar regulation and supports ligaments, discs and bones. In excess, however, manganese can be toxic because it depletes the neurotransmitter dopamine which effects mental functioning.

Used as an antiknock component in gasoline, manganese is also found in inks, dyes, glass, paint, varnish, matches, fireworks and metal alloys. Skin absorption from gasoline causes bleeding, swelling, kidney and nerve damage, hyperactivity, convulsions and coma.

People who have been exposed for extended periods to this metal's fumes and dust are liable to develop "manganese madness." The initial symptoms include exhaustion, a trancelike hypnotic state, tremendous irritability and erratic behavior with wild emotional swings, hallucinations and impotence. Some develop symptoms resembling those of Parkinson's disease.

Mercury

Nearly 50 years ago, the ravages of mercury brought worldwide attention to the dangers of this heavy metal in the environment. In the 1950s, more than 100 people died in the Japanese town of Minamata after eating fish with high flesh levels of mercury from industrial effluents into the bay. Thousands more suffered brain and nerve damage or gave birth to handicapped children.

A less publicized but even greater disaster took place in Iraq in December 1971, when a shipload of Mexican seed grain treated with a mercury-containing fungicide was eaten instead of planted. About 460 people died, and another 6,530 people suffered damage to their nervous systems. Historically, the phrase "mad as a hatter" refers to the occupational risk of mercury vapor to London hatters in the 1800s. Venetian glass makers suffered similar risks.

The death of the 48-year-old American research chemist Karen Wetterhahn was an extreme case, but one which vividly illustrates the power of mercury toxicity and brings the danger even closer to home. In an experiment at Dartmouth College in New Hampshire, she was working with the very toxic compound dimethylmercury. On August 14, 1996, a couple of drops of this compound fell on her latex glove. She quickly wiped them away, but the toxin had already penetrated the latex and her skin. Five months later, her gait began to falter and she started to slur words. She gradually became blind, deaf and dumb before lapsing into a coma. She died in June 1997, less than a year after the lab accident. Dimethylmercury is a rare compound and far more toxic than most other mercury compounds. Yet Karen, a distinguished scientist and a world expert on the dangers of heavy metals, had not realized how dangerous this compound actually was.

A major risk in our surroundings today is in the form of organometallic compounds. Mercury in polluted air and seawater combines with organic compounds in the environment to form dangerous new organometallic molecules. The complex ways in which these molecules interact with and cause damage to human, animal and plant life are only now becoming fully understood. Inorganic mercury compounds, however, remain relatively abundant in the environment. They are used in dental amalgams, fungicides and antiseptics. They are also found in the flesh of large fish, such as swordfish and tuna (albacore tuna has the lowest levels). Painters, potters, metalworkers, jewelers and photo developers often have dangerous exposure to mercury.

It Is All in Your Head

My personal concerns about the health risks of mercury (particularly those of mercury amalgams in my own mouth) began in February of 1974 when I attended my first class with Dr. Hazel Parcells. At that time, Dr. Parcells explained that, based upon her extensive research and testing, mercury was an unsafe substance for dental fillings because it affects the production of the neurotransmitter serotonin in the brain. (Amazingly, these findings were substantiated nearly 20 years later in breakthrough research at the Rocky Mountain Research Institute led by Robert L. Siblerud.) Dr. Parcells told me that she personally felt that my own "artistic" personality and quicksilver mind were in large part due to the large number of mercury fillings in my mouth—nine, to be exact. Needless to say, early on I got on the antimercury bandwagon and, over the past two decades, have had all my amalgams removed and replaced with an inert, nonreactive plastic material.

Here's the source of the problem. Dental fillings called amalgams are made up mostly of mercury (50 percent), silver, copper and tin. "For the longest time," states Dr. Thomas Levy, Director of Peak Energy Performance in Colorado Springs, "it was simply asserted by the American Dental Association that the mercury amalgam was a tightly bound complex that would not permit any leakage or release of mercury. This was proved conclusively wrong by Vimy and Lorscheider in 1985 when they demonstrated that the air inside the mouth with amalgams continually contained elemental mercury vapor, and the dynamic of chewing increased this vapor level substantially."

As mercury expert Dr. Hal Huggins writes in his booklet *Serum Compatibility Testing: A Crucial Methodology for Modern Dentistry,* ". . . many diseases and symptoms of diseases have responded to the removal of mercury, copper and tin-containing fillings called amalgams. Many of these diseases were termed autoimmune diseases or diseases in which one's immune system turned against its own tissues and began to destroy itself. Some of these diseases are arthritis, multiple sclerosis, lupus erythematosis and numerous others symptomatic of autoimmune diseases."

To determine the frequency of symptom occurrence, over 1,300 patients were interviewed by Dr. Huggins with a lengthy questionnaire. Their responses were tabulated and symptoms of systemic autoimmune responses listed.

Frequency of Symptoms in Those with Mercury Amalgam Fillings

Symptom	Percentage
Unexplained irritability	73.3
Constant or very frequent periods of depression	72.0
Numbness and tingling in extremities	67.3
Frequent urination during the night	64.5
Unexplained chronic fatigue	63.1
Cold hands and feet even in moderate or warm weather	62.6
Bloated feeling most of the time	60.6
Difficulty remembering or use of memory	58.0
Sudden, unexplained or unsolicited anger	55.5
Constipation on a regular basis	54.6
Twitching of face and other muscles	52.3
Difficulty in making even simple decisions	54.2
Frequent leg cramps	49.1

Constant or frequent ringing or noise in ears	47.8
Breathlessness	43.1
Frequent or recurring heartburn	42.5
Excessive itching	40.8
Unexplained rashes, skin irritation	40.4
Constant or frequent metallic taste in mouth	38.7
Jumpy, jittery, nervous behavior	38.1
Constant death wish or suicidal intent	37.3
Frequent insomnia	36.4
Unexplained chest pains	35.6
Constant or frequent pain in joints	35.5
Tachycardia	32.4
Tremors or shakiness of hands, feet, head, etc.	31.8
Unexplained fluid retention	28.2
Burning sensation on the tongue	20.8
Headaches after eating	20.1
Frequent diarrhea	14.9

Europeans have taken the lead in protecting their citizens from the hazards of mercury amalgams. In the early 1990s, the German Health Ministry recommended to the German Dental Association that amalgam fillings not be used for children, pregnant women and people with kidney disease. In December 1993, this recommendation was extended to include all women of child-bearing age, whether pregnant or not. Because of legal concerns, Germany's largest manufacturer of amalgam ceased production shortly after. Sweden banned the use of amalgam fillings for children and young adults in June 1995 and for everybody in January 1997, claiming that a quarter-million Swedes already had immune and other health disorders that could be linked to amalgam fillings. Denmark plans to ban them as of January 1999.

Sadly, the official American stand is quite different. The American Dental Association's 1994 *Code of Professional Conduct* states that it is "improper and unethical" for a dentist to recommend replacement of mercury amalgams to a nonallergenic patient. Keep this in mind when discussing this matter with your regular dentist.

Nickel

Water, air, soil and food can be contaminated with nickel compounds due to the manufacturing of steel, batteries, machine parts, wiring and electrical parts. Fats and oils hydrogenated with nickel catalysts can also be contaminated. Poor quality stainless steel cookware leaches nickel into food being cooked. People who work with pottery pigments, enamel and varnish, along with glassblowers and metalworkers, often are exposed to nickel compounds.

Nickel, which tends to accumulate in the kidneys, interferes with hormone production. Symptoms include low blood pressure, nausea, gastric pain and lethargy as well as kidney dysfunction.

Selenium

Selenium is a helpful antioxidant in small quantities, functioning in conjunction with vitamin E. But, in excess this metal is toxic. A pollutant of air and water, it can pass through the placenta to an unborn infant. Jewelers, painters, glassblowers and photo developers are also often exposed to this metal. However, selenium is increasingly being taken in excess through supplements. One of my own clients, for example, was exhibiting classic symptoms of osteoporosis. Yet blood mineral testing found her levels of bone-building calcium and magnesium as well as manganese and zinc quite adequate. It was only after I suggested she take a tissue

mineral analysis through a hair sample that the problem was identified. Her selenium was off the charts. We then went through all
her various dietary supplements (she was taking much more than
a handful) and discovered, quite shockingly, that her daily selenium intake of 1,000 mcg far exceeded the recommended amount
of 200–250 mcg daily.

A puffy reddening of the eyelids, called rose eyes, horizontal
white streaks on the nails, inflammation of the skin around the
nails and a garlic odor on the breath are characteristic symptoms
of long-term exposure.

Silver

A primary ingredient in mercury amalgams, silver is used in an
array of products, from medicines through jewelry to film. Silver
can cause reduced night vision in those who work with it for an
extended period. Skin contact with silver can result in gray or
blue-black discoloration of the skin as well as skin, mouth, eye
and nose irritation. Swallowing silver nitrate causes blackening
and pain of the mouth and throat, black vomit, lack of urine, diarrhea, shock, convulsions, coma and death. Even overuse of the
highly touted colloidal silver may be unwise because this so-
called natural antibiotic can wipe out the body's intestinal flora—
the bad flora as well as the good.

Vanadium

This metal, taken as a trace mineral, can be therapeutic in minute
dosages for diabetics, body builders and all those seeking blood

sugar regulation. Metalworkers, potters, painters, printers, gardeners, photographers and textile dyers are likely to be exposed to heavy doses of this metal, with irritation of the eyes and respiratory tract occurring which can lead to bronchitis or pneumonia.

Zinc

A vitally important nutrient, zinc acts as an insulin potentiator, fortifier of the immune system and bone builder. In excess, however, zinc is toxic even when taken in supplemental form. The metal is used in many industrial alloys and for galvanizing steel and iron. Its two most common compounds in everyday life are zinc oxide and zinc chloride. Zinc oxide, which is not very soluble in water, is found in sunblock creams, paints, varnishes, lacquers and various drugs and chemicals. Zinc chloride, soluble in water, is used in wood preservatives, deodorants, disinfectants, dyes and batteries. Potters, jewelers, painters and glassblowers are liable to be exposed to excess amounts of the metal.

Zinc toxicity via the supplemental route can result in a lowering of the HDL ("good" cholesterol) when amounts exceed 50 mg on a long-term daily basis. Environmental long-term exposure to zinc does not seem to cause as intense symptoms as other toxic metals. Zinc oxide causes itchy red pustules on the skin, called oxide pox. Zinc chloride is more toxic. It corrodes the skin and internal organs, sometimes causing death through damage to the lungs. Gastric pain and vomiting of blood are typical symptoms.

What You Can Do to Metal-proof Your Life

Tissue mineral analysis of hair is one of the most sensitive and inexpensive indicators of exposure to heavy metals. While toxic metal exposure can also be detected through special blood and urine testing, a hair sample provides a three-month metabolic blueprint. Moreover, a hair sample does not involve invasive testing or a doctor's prescription. Although some professionals dismiss hair analysis as unreliable, I have always found it to be a reliable and predictive measure of mineral levels and patterns of health. In fact, many times toxicity from heavy metals shows up on the hair long before elevated levels are detected in the blood or urine. Hair analysis is a reliable heavy-metal screen when you consider that hair follicles are washed by blood, lymph and extra-cellular fluids that deposit tiny fragments of any metal contaminants they contain. As the hair emerges from its follicle, it hardens and fossilizes the metabolic products within it. Tissue mineral analysis uses this record to show what toxic metals you have been exposed to (such as arsenic, mercury, cadmium, lead and aluminum) as well as the current levels and ratios of nutrient minerals like calcium, magnesium, potassium, manganese, sodium, iron, zinc and copper.

The specific treatment for heavy-metal toxicity varies based upon the testing results. For example, most hair analysis reports contain a nutrition supplement program specifically designed to balance biochemistry. This program is generally followed for a two-to-three-month period after which a retest is recommended to monitor progress. If you would like to screen for possible toxic metal buildup and would like a tissue mineral analysis of a hair sample, call Uni Key Health Systems (see Resources).

Provocative chelation can also be used as a testing procedure for heavy metals. This procedure consists of the administration of chelators or binders, such as the intravenously given EDTA (ethylene diamine tetra-acetic acid), dimercoprol/DMPS (usually administered as a shot) or the oral d-penicillamine. These substances bind with toxic metals in the tissues for excretion in the blood and urine. Urine is then collected in a special container for 24 hours, after which a portion is sent to a lab for analysis. For the name of a physician in your area who practices chelation therapy call the American College for Advancement in Medicine (see Resources).

The amino acid N-acetylcysteine (NAC) taken in the amount of 500 mg, one to two times daily and methionine (500 mg), taken two times daily have been shown to have broad-based chelating effects for just about every metal. The same can be said for the antioxidants, such as vitamin C (2,000 mg) taken three or more times per day, vitamin E (400 I.U.), taken one to three times per day, glutathione (150–300 mg per day) and beta carotene (25,000–50,000 I.U. per day).

In addition to a special nutritional supplement program, a high-fiber diet (25–35 grams) is a helpful aid to tie up metals and excrete them from the system. A diet high in legumes, pectin (in the form of apples), seaweeds (kombu, nori, hijiki and sea palms) and flaxseed meal is both naturally chelating, laxative and lubricating.

Finally, if you suspect aluminum, mercury, lead or arsenic toxicity, try a Parcells' therapeutic bath for heavy metals once or twice a week. Add one cup of Clorox brand bleach (blue and white label) to a tub of very hot water. Soak in the bathtub until the water cools. Do not take a shower for at least four hours after this cleansing bath.

ALUMINUM SOLUTIONS

To aluminum-proof your life, remove as many aluminum sources as possible, including pots, pans, aluminum foil, deodorants and antacids. Consider a lifetime investment for health by purchasing the waterless cooking and vacuum-sealed Royal Prestige Cookware by West Bend. Royal Prestige is a 7-ply nonreactive titanium steel with unsurpassed durability and heating efficiency. Taking 400–800 mg magnesium can also be helpful as it is the mineral antagonist to aluminum.

COPPER SOLUTIONS

To copper-proof your life, remove as many copper sources as possible, including copper pots and pans, copper IUDs, copper dental materials, and filter copper out of your water through the Doulton or other water filtration systems. If a hair analysis shows you are copper-toxic, seek out copper-free vitamin and mineral preparations and avoid copper-rich foods such as soy products, shellfish, tea, chocolate and wheat bran. Zinc supplements act to balance out copper because zinc is the mineral antagonist to copper.

IRON SOLUTIONS

To iron-proof your life, stay away from all iron-enriched cereals and flours which are then made into baked goods. Eliminate red meat, beans and molasses from your life. Become a label reader. Unless a blood test shows you are anemic, stay away from all vitamin and mineral supplements that contain extra iron. Also, remember that vitamin C enhances iron absorption. Monitor your levels of stored iron on a yearly basis with a ferritin test, especially if you are a male over the age of 40 and heart disease runs in the family. If you are a female and have stopped menstruating, now is the time for a baseline ferritin level, too. If iron levels are high, consider becoming a regular blood donor. This releases iron from your body.

LEAD SOLUTIONS

To lead-proof your life, or especially your child's life, keep him or her away from lead-based paint chips. Use a water filter to remove lead in the home. Extra calcium may be in order because calcium is the mineral antagonist to lead. If you want to test your antique china pattern for possible lead contamination, you can order a lead-testing kit from the Environmental Defense Fund (see Resources).

MERCURY SOLUTIONS

To mercury-proof your life, stay away from large fish such as tuna and swordfish as well as medications like Preparation H, certain contact lens solutions, diuretics and Mercurochrome.

Consider taking some selenium (no more than 200 mcg), as this is the mineral antagonist to mercury.

If you have amalgam fillings and are concerned about their effect on your health, contact Peak Energy Performance (see Resources). They can direct you to a practitioner of mercury-free dentistry who has trained under Hal Huggins, D.D.S., the acknowledged expert in biological dentistry and proper amalgam removal.

Peak Energy Performance provides serum-compatibility testing, which not only tests for reactivity to amalgam components (like mercury, copper, zinc and silver), but also tests for biocompatability to plastic filling materials which can contain a variety of reactive substances like toluene, acrylates and antimony. Over 750 dental materials are evaluated, such as cements, glue, sealants, adhesives and even root canal materials.

Dental biocompatability testing practically saved my life. Through it, I learned how reactive I was not just to the mercury in my amalgams but also to the aluminum used in my porcelain caps and the copper in my gold fillings.

6
Radiation:
Toxic Invader #4

"In many respects, radiation is the greatest contaminant in the world. It cannot be seen, felt or heard. It is tasteless and odorless. It is in our food and in the air; it is in our blood and in our bones and can remain in our ashes to go on to contaminate someone else." So wrote Sara Shannon in *Diet for the Atomic Age.*

Radiation damages living tissue by removing electrons from other atoms or molecules with which it comes into contact. These radioactive particles get into our bodies via air, water or food, destroying tissues and organs, cells and genes, Shannon explains.

According to Dr. Parcells, natural low-level radiation has been around in the environment for years. And for years we lived harmoniously with it. Then, in the late 19th century, X-rays were discovered, and their use has escalated tremendously since the 1930s. The corresponding increase of other sources of low-level radiation—including the use of all kinds of microwave and electronic equipment, not to mention nuclear power—has pumped tremendous amounts of radioactivity into the environment. And it doesn't just stay in one place. Because radioactivity is airborne, it can be transported for hundreds of miles beyond its origin. For example, Dr. Parcells could detect radioactivity in the air at her center in Albuquerque that had originated in Los Angeles.

Dr. Parcells believed that the effects of radiation on our health were horrendous. It shortens our life span. It can cause premature aging, cancer, leukemia, genetic mutations, abnormal blood clotting, thyroid dysfunction and numerous other health problems. It can create mental impairment and fetal and infant deaths. It zaps our immune system, leaving us vulnerable to all sorts of nonspecific ailments from mysterious viruses to attacks of the so-called "flu." If we could see the invisible clouds of radiation which are especially concentrated in heavily populated and industrial areas, we would be horrified. The air we inhale and expose our bodies to every day is becoming a kind of chemical soup. We are being poisoned by radiation on the job, at home, or while flying in an airplane. Smokers inhale and exhale concentrated radiation with their tobacco; secondhand smoke contains radioactivity. Proximity to nuclear power plants and concentrated sources of microwave energy make us vulnerable to radiation poisoning. Leakage from underground nuclear testing creates diluted fallout that can dissipate throughout the environment.

Radiation does its damage by entering the body and attaching to the cells where it stays for a very long time, absorbing large amounts of minerals and trace elements, leaving the body with little reserve to carry on its normal functions of digestion, absorption, elimination and reproduction.

The Electromagnetic Spectrum

The sound of a bell, the heat from a flame, a TV transmitter's invisible signal and visible light from a distant star are all different forms of the same thing—the radiation of energy. The various forms of radiant energy can be classified according to the number of wavelengths at which they travel per second. Sound travels the slowest, and cosmic rays the fastest. Between slowest and fastest, the various kinds of energy can be arranged along an electromagnetic spectrum in which faster (shorter) wavelengths carry more energy.

Approximate positions of various kinds of radiation on the electromagnetic spectrum allow energy to liberate electrons and damage the molecular structure of cells, often resulting in pathological changes. It is generally accepted that high doses or prolonged exposure to ionizing radiation (X-rays, gamma rays, cosmic rays) are a direct cause of cancer.

Because of their lower energy (slower or longer wavelengths), radiant energy from ultraviolet through visible light, infrared, microwave, radio and sound are known as nonionizing radiation. Although nonionizing radiation cannot cause cell damage at the level of, say, gamma rays from a nuclear device, it can be extremely dangerous for many reasons. The less widely known dangers of both ionizing and nonionizing radiation pose the greatest everyday threat to our health. The threat lies more in our failure to recognize the risk than in the energy level of the radiation source itself, as we will see in the studies that follow.

Electromagnetic Fields

In the United States, alternating current flows in opposite directions at a rate of 60 cycles per second (in Europe, it is 50). The electric and magnetic fields produced by the alternating current are together called electromagnetic fields (EMFs). Considering that the earth has an apparently harmless magnetic field, EMFs were thought not to contain enough energy to harm human tissue.

In 1979, Nancy Wertheimer and Edward Leeper published a study on children in Denver who had died of leukemia between 1950 and 1973. They found that a significant number of the houses in which the children had lived were situated near power cables or transformers. Their study suggested that children living within the EMFs produced by these cables and transformers were twice as likely to die of leukemia as other children. A 1986 follow-up study, led by David Savitz of the University of Colorado Medical School, reviewed factors other than EMFs that might have affected the children's health, such as their exposure to pesticides or X-rays, and confirmed the fact that children who lived close to power lines were more likely to die of leukemia.

The 1979 study and others that soon followed caused consternation in the utility industry. It was not hard to see why. More than 350,000 miles of high-voltage power lines carry electricity around the nation. About two million additional miles of cable carry lower-voltage electricity from high-voltage lines to users. Nearly all these lines are capable of producing EMFs at the relatively low levels thought to have harmed the Denver children.

The New York State Power Lines Project was the largest of several ensuing state-sponsored studies. While the study reported that EMFs can affect the human body, it played down the need for major change. In a policy followed by other states, New York State decided that future power lines could not emit EMFs stronger than those from lines already in existence. This compromise helped calm the public without committing the utility industry to new construction or more rigorous safety standards. The fact that a public health problem exists with the power lines already in place has been more or less suppressed or ignored—and herein lies the major risk to our health.

A 1989 Carnegie Mellon University report for the congressional Office of Technology Assessment claimed that while EMFs could no longer be called risk-free, they had not been shown to have a significant risk. Presumably, if more children had died, the risk would have grown in significance. A 1990 EPA draft report cited links between EMFs and leukemia, lymphoma and brain cancer in children. It was reviewed by the EPA in 1991 and judged to be too strongly stated.

Yet the flow of clinical observations and research reports supporting links between EMFs and cancer continued. The Electric Power Research Institute released a study in 1991 that associated leukemia in children with nearby power lines and the use of TV sets, hair dryers and other household electrical appliances. The biggest study was published in Sweden in 1992. It involved all children with cancer and all adults with leukemia or brain cancer, diagnosed between 1960 and 1985, among nearly 500,000 people who lived within a hundred yards of medium- and high-voltage power lines in Sweden. Significant links between EMFs and such cancers were found, and later acknowledged by the Swedish National Board for Industrial and Technical Development. A similar acknowledgment has not been forthcoming from any U.S. federal or state agency or industrial authority.

For American adults, most of the evidence of EMF-cancer links comes from occupational studies, especially from industrial work involving high-voltage electricity. But high energy is not the chief danger factor with adults, nor was it for children. This has been demonstrated by a continuing Johns Hopkins University study of 50,000 men working for the New York phone company. Telephones require only a very low voltage. Cable splicers, the workers with the greatest exposure to EMFs, are seven times more likely to develop leukemia than workers with no exposure to EMFs. The high-exposure workers also develop more prostate, lung, lymph and colon cancers than nonexposed workers.

Electrical conduits inside the walls of buildings generate EMFs. With the spread of computers and electronic communications, the space above the false ceiling of many offices contains sheaves of electrical cables running in all directions. In addition to

EMFs generated above their heads office workers in high-rise buildings are subjected continuously and simultaneously to many forms of radiation from other directions. To believe that this prolonged irradiation is harmless to one's health requires an optimism bordering on the reckless.

Electrical Appliances and Microwave Ovens

Besides generating EMFs, many household electrical appliances emit dangerous amounts of nonionizing radiation, particularly electric razors, hair dryers and power tools. They are considered safe for consumer use only because they are utilized for short periods. Keeping this fact in mind can protect you. For example, an electric blanket gives out much the same EMFs as an electric toaster or alarm clock. The chances are that you don't spend much time in close proximity to your electric toaster and, hopefully, your electric alarm clock is at least a couple of feet from your body while you sleep. But sleeping all night under an electric blanket generating EMFs is a very different matter and has been reported to be dangerous. Switching the blanket off before you go to bed eliminates the danger.

As microwaves generated inside an oven ricochet off its interior walls, they repeatedly pass through the food in the oven and agitate its water molecules. The friction of this agitation generates heat, and the heat cooks the food. No radioactivity is present to contaminate the food, but leakage of microwaves around the doors of defective or old ovens can be dangerous at short range (within inches). Keep at least a few feet away from a working oven to protect yourself.

Living Near Nuclear Facilities

Millions of Americans live within 100 miles of a nuclear power station or military facility where nuclear weapons have been manufactured, stored or even tested. Using official data from the CDC, National Cancer Institute and state health departments, radiation expert Jay M. Gould examined the health consequences of living within 100 miles of a nuclear facility. In 1996, he published his findings in *The Enemy Within*. Among the more striking of his discoveries was the fact that in the time it took the national rate of breast cancer incidence to double, the rate quintupled in the 14 counties with the longest history of nuclear reactors. He also found that people who lived near nuclear facilities were more vulnerable to immune deficiencies and AIDS. Additionally, babies born near a nuclear facility are more likely to be premature and underweight.

In reviewing this book in *The Nation* magazine, Blanche Wiesen Cook noted that she herself lives in the area with the highest rate of breast cancer in the United States—the east end of Long Island. Not coincidentally, there are three Millstone nuclear reactors in this area which have never become operational because of safety violations, and two small reactors at the Brookhaven National Laboratory which have discharged radioactive iodine, strontium and tritium into the air and a local river for 45 years.

In his book, Gould discusses how, in 1945, the Hanford nuclear weapons complex in Washington state released radioactive iodine into the atmosphere that rivaled in magnitude that released in Chernobyl in 1986. On May 14, 1997, less than a year after his book was published, the latest in a series of nuclear accidents at Hanford occurred when a steel tank inside an airtight building exploded and released a brown toxic cloud through a crack in the roof. The escaped gas was not radioactive. This was fortunate, because the people in charge placed secrecy before public health, allowing three hours to elapse before notifying state officials and refusing entrance to a radiation survey team for four hours.

Symptoms of Radiation Poisoning

Our reproductive organs, bone marrow, lymph system, skin and mucous membranes are the parts of our body most sensitive to radiation. We are so often assured that the radiation we receive is harmless and has no ill effects that it is reasonable to wonder what the initial symptoms of radiation poisoning would be. Dr. Parcells believed that symptoms such as nausea, fatigue that no rest could alleviate, headaches, jet lag discomforts, dizziness and general muscle aches and pains were all connected to radiation as well. Interestingly, these are similar to the side effects that the American Cancer Society warns patients about who receive radiation therapy.

Fatigue. The most frequent symptoms of radiation poisoning are tiredness and lethargy. While it is not known for certain why this occurs, it may be due to the body's using up energy in repairing damaged tissue. It may also be due to a buildup of toxic wastes in the body as a result of cell damage and breakdown. A speeding up of cell metabolism is another possible explanation for the feelings of fatigue.

Loss of appetite. This is another typical symptom of radiation poisoning. Changes in cell chemistry may interfere with the hormones that control the body's hunger signal. A loss of some sense of taste may make food seem less palatable. Feelings of stress may also be a factor.

Skin problems. Reddening of the skin, along with dryness and itchiness, are typical skin conditions caused by radiation. They are usually localized to the part of the body affected by the radiation. Less frequently, the skin may actually peel. In the rare condition of moist desquamation, skin folds become wet and sore.

When radiation affects a single area of the body, as it usually does in cancer therapy, characteristic symptoms can appear. For example, radiation of the stomach often causes nausea and vomiting. Radiation of the head and neck often causes the mouth's mucous membranes to redden. The person may also suffer from extreme dryness of the mouth and lips, have a shortage of saliva, lose his or her sense of taste and have difficulty swallowing.

What You Can Do to Eliminate and Protect against Radiation

Dr. Parcells recommended a sea salt and soda bath for neutralizing radiation exposures from X-rays, fallout, nuclear plant emissions and plane travel. Draw a bathtub full of medium hot water and add two cups of sea salt and two cups of baking soda. Soak for about 20 minutes or until the water cools. If you are living at least 50 miles from a nuclear plant, it is suggested that you take a salt and soda bath at least twice a week. It is particularly helpful after rain, snow or fog when the radioactive particles are brought closer to the ground. To retain the therapeutic effects, do not shower after the bath.

In severe cases of radiation exposure, Dr. Parcells recommended the following special daily drink: one teaspoon each baking soda and sea salt dissolved in one quart of distilled water. Take one 8-ounce glass every hour for the first two doses; then space the next two doses two hours apart. If more is needed, space the doses three hours apart until all symptoms are gone.

Food substances like bee pollen, bee propolis, dried primary grown nutritional yeast, lecithin, thymus extract, cysteine, pectin, charcoal and germanium all help the body fight off the ravages of radiation. Specialty foods such as sea vegetables, with their high sodium alginate content, are also good radiation chelators. Other helpful sea vegetables are nori, hijiki and chlorella. Miso soup is also a known radiation protector.

Homeopathic cell salts also counter radiation. The 6x potency of all 12 cell salts can be taken under the tongue several times a day. Kali phos seems to be the most effective of all the tissue mineral salts for this purpose.

Herbal aid from astragalus, ginseng and shiitake and maitake mushrooms can also fight radiation.

Heavy-duty antioxidants such as glutathione, catalase, lipoic acid, grape seed extract, pine bark and vitamins A, E and C will assist in mopping up free radical damage created by the radiation molecules.

A BioElectric Shield can be worn to protect the body against the electromagnetic energy fields surrounding electrical equipment, fluorescent lighting and power lines. Uni Key provides a homeopathic formula that helps to eliminate radiation from the system caused by power plants, electromagnetics from computers, airplane travel and X-rays. I use this formula on a daily basis, especially when traveling (see Resources).

7

Detoxifying Your Indoor Air Environment

The air we breathe, like the food we eat and the water we drink, is simply nonnegotiable for health and well-being. Let's remember that we can survive several days without food and water, but only ten minutes without air. The air we breathe must be clean and free of pollutants so that it can provide life-supporting and life-enhancing oxygen that will keep us young and vital. Air, which is made up of oxygen, nitrogen, carbon dioxide, water vapors and trace gases, is a precious mixture essential to life itself.

Sadly, pure air, like untainted food and water, is practically extinct on planet Earth these days. The outdoor air contains auto exhaust, industrial and agricultural chemicals and numerous other toxic products. In fact, the American Lung Association states that nearly 160 million Americans in over 180 urban areas are breathing air deemed "unhealthy" by the Environmental Protection Agency. In addition to the toxic pollutants from industry and motor vehicles, the protective ozone layer is deteriorating on a daily basis, increasing our risk for skin cancer. Due to extreme ozone depletion, ultraviolet radiation has now penetrated our oceans and created genetic damage at the very source of our food chain—the marine-based organisms called phytoplankton.

As unbelievable as it may sound, we are more likely to get sick from the indoor air in our home or office than from the outdoor air. According to the Environmental Protection Agency, indoor air pollution is one of the leading health risks in the environment. In fact, some chemicals may be nearly 100 times more concentrated indoors than outdoors. Since many Americans spend as much as 90 percent of their time indoors, we need to readjust our viewpoint of environmental degradation as an outdoor event. You don't have to leave home to find it.

Dr. Bill Wolverton, retired NASA research scientist, concurs. In his book *How to Grow Clean Air: 50 Houseplants That Purify Your Home or Office,* he writes, "We are used to thinking of the indoor environment as a safe haven from the evils of air pollution. During smog alerts people are generally advised to stay indoors. Yet modern scientific research indicates that the indoor environment may be as much as ten times more polluted than the outdoor environment." Plain and simple, the typical American home is not one of the healthiest places to live anymore, what with radon, asbestos, formaldehyde, mold, mildew and all the household chemicals, carpeting, rugs and furnishings you are likely to find there today.

More efficient building techniques have created tighter, better-insulated homes and offices with increased heating and cooling economy. Indoor air contaminants can lethally accumulate in a "tight" house or office building. For this reason, it is very important to monitor air quality. Even though pure air both outdoors and indoors is fast becoming a dinosaur on the planet, there are many lifestyle changes we can make on an individual basis to do the best we can to assure the purity of the indoor air we breathe. First, let's discuss the most prevalent sources of indoor pollution and then review what we can do to tackle the toxins, simply, easily and naturally.

Radon: Natural-born Killer

The health risk from radon is not news. What is newsworthy is that Americans apparently refuse to take this seriously. Radon is a naturally occurring invisible and odorless gas that comes from soil or rock containing uranium. Radon gas seeps into a house from rocks and soil, through pores and cracks in the foundation, slab-footing joints, mortar joints and loose-fitting pipes.

Radon contamination is more likely in homes with basements than those that have slab foundations. This is also more likely to accumulate in a "tight" home that has been insulated for energy efficiency. According to the National Academy of Sciences data, radon is responsible for 55 percent of the ionizing radiation that Americans are exposed to. Up to 30,000 Americans die each year from lung cancer attributed to radon exposure. The radon breaks down into harmful radioactive elements that attach to dust particles and can enter the lungs. There the elements further decay, destroying surrounding cells which can eventually lead to cancer.

Radon can be found nearly everywhere in the United States. An Environmental Protection Agency (EPA) Survey of 11,000 homes in seven states found threatening levels of radon in nearly one-third of the homes. The following figures represent the percentage of homes in each state studied with unsafe levels of radon:

North Dakota - 63%
Minnesota - 46%
Pennsylvania - 37%
Indiana - 26%
Massachusetts - 24%
Missouri - 18%
Arizona - 8%

According to the EPA and the New Jersey State Health Department estimates, almost one-third of northern New Jersey homes have sufficient radon seeped into their basements to pose a greater than 1 in 100 lifetime risk of lung cancer. The panic expected when this news was released never materialized. In fact, less than 5 percent of the affected homeowners bothered to obtain the low-cost radon monitors made available to them.

This lack of concern is at least partly explained by the fact that radon is a natural product rather than a manufactured one. Researcher Peter Sandman pointed out that when three New Jersey communities discovered that they were being exposed to radon from an industrial landfill, they demanded action on the state level despite the fact that the landfill radon levels were no higher than those in many homes. When the state offered merely to dilute the landfill levels to local natural levels, major environmental protests followed.

The Pennsylvania Bureau of Radiation Protection estimated that more than 10,000 people in that state are exposed to radon levels 25 times the highest acceptable limit within a home and that more than 180,000 homes have radon levels 5 times the highest acceptable level. Dangerous radon levels have been found in every state in which tests have been conducted. The EPA estimated that 6 percent of American homes have radon levels high enough to be dangerous to occupants. I believe that the number may be higher, much higher.

Asbestos: From Miracle Material to Hazardous Waste

Once regarded as a miracle material, asbestos is now known as a potential health hazard. Like radon, it is a naturally occurring substance. Asbestos was valued for its extraordinary fireproofing and insulating qualities. Any home built between 1945 and 1970 probably contains asbestos somewhere. It is found in ceiling and floor tiles, pipes, ceiling and wall insulation, around furnaces, in vinyl sheet flooring, roof and siding shingles, paints and joint compounds.

When asbestos fibers become airborne and build up in the lungs, they can cause lung cancer and scarring in the lungs. Asbestos has also been linked to stomach cancer. It can take from 15 to 35 years before symptoms even show themselves. Most asbestos-related cancer cases have occurred from work-related exposure.

The good news is that asbestos in the house doesn't necessarily mean there is a problem unless the fibers are released. This happens when the asbestos begins to break down or starts to flake off. Luckily, the federal government has banned most asbestos products.

Formaldehyde: The Ever-present Indoor Toxin

Formaldehyde is absolutely everywhere! For most of us it is virtually impossible to avoid the chemical formaldehyde. Composed of carbon, hydrogen and oxygen, it is released naturally by plants, animals and humans. Coal, oil and cars as well as cigarettes and gas give off formaldehyde. The permanent press in clothes and sheets is due to the presence of formaldehyde. It is in many cosmetics such as lipstick, shampoo and even toothpaste. It can be found in paper towels (giving them their wet strength), disposable sanitary products and facial tissues. Formaldehyde is used as a bonding agent in a huge number of consumer products. It is used in products as diverse as disinfectants, electrical equipment, countertops and car bodies.

Most health problems arise when the formaldehyde incompletely bonds with the product in which it is used. Incomplete bonding results in formaldehyde leaking, which most often occurs when products are new, particularly from furniture like bookcases and cabinets made from plywood or particle board. subflooring, drapes, upholstery and carpeting. Besides building materials, furniture and carpeting, urea formaldehyde foam insulation (BUFFI) is another source of formaldehyde.

When the need for energy conservation became a national concern in the 1970s, many people used urea foam formaldehyde insulation to further insulate their walls. In 1982, the U.S. Consumer Products Safety Commission banned urea formaldehyde insulation because of thousands of consumer complaints of toxic reactions. This ban has been overturned since, but it is still in effect in several states.

Modern apartments and condos fall into especially high levels of formaldehyde outgassing because of the extensive use of pre-built cabinets and factory-produced building materials to speed up construction. Mobile homes can also contain large quantities of formaldehyde in the walls, floors and cabinets because of the prevalent use of pressed-wood building materials and synthetic carpets. Fumes become concentrated due to the small air space. Since February 1985, manufacturers have been required by law to display formaldehyde health warnings in newly built mobile homes. The warnings state that "elderly persons and young children and anyone with a history of asthma, allergies or lung problems may be at greater risk."

Outgassing from formaldehyde in mobile homes, new homes and products can cause irritation of the eyes, nose, ears and throat as well as nosebleeds, nausea, headaches and dizziness. It has a particular picklelike odor. When you start smelling that pungent odor, it is a clue to begin to check for formaldehyde.

Carbon Monoxide: The Silent Killer

Carbon monoxide, along with nitrogen dioxide and sulpha dioxide are the toxic by-products of gas combustion. Life-threatening levels of all these gases can build up from poorly ventilated furnaces, gas, oil or coal stoves, kerosene heaters and clothes dryers. Gas stoves present the most severe carbon monoxide problems because even ventilation does not totally eliminate the released toxic gas. Besides gas stoves, the automobile is a major producer of carbon monoxide. The gas becomes concentrated when cars are warmed up or left idling in closed garages. Carbon monoxide can leak into the car or into the house if the garage is attached.

Carbon monoxide binds with the blood's hemoglobin, thus reducing oxygen in the body. Excessive exposure can cause asphyxiation. Long-term exposure has been known to create nausea, confusion, fatigue, headaches, lack of coordination and dizziness. Oftentimes drowsiness in one's house can be related to working too closely to the stove. In fact, even mental problems that have necessitated psychiatric intervention have been traced to gas leaks in the home.

CIGARETTE SMOKING: WHEN SMOKE GETS IN MORE THAN YOUR EYES

Cigarette smoke also releases carbon monoxide. In fact, smoking can create indoor levels of carbon monoxide that far exceed the federal air quality standard levels for outside air. Cigars produce twice as much carbon monoxide as three cigarettes smoked simultaneously. According to the American Heart and Lung Association, tobacco smoke enters our air from two sources: sidestream or secondhand smoke which is from a burning cigarette and mainstream smoke which is the smoke the smoker inhales. Nonsmokers are exposed to both sidestream smoke and mainstream smoke after the smoker exhales it. Sidestream smoke has higher concentrations of noxious compounds than the mainstream smoke inhaled by the smoker, according to the American Lung Association.

After being exposed to tobacco smoke, carbon monoxide in the blood causes impaired driving performance, impaired ability to judge time and impaired performance on psychomotor tests. Secondhand smoke can also trigger asthma attacks in children as well as eye irritation, headaches, coughs and nasal discomfort.

Have you ever wondered why your skin and clothes smell like cigarette smoke after being with a smoker? The human body appears to attract cigarette smoke. Smoke clings to people much the same way iron fillings are drawn to a magnet. The chemicals in tobacco, particularly aldehydes and ketones, create the penetrating smell, while the tars in the cigarette hold the smell to your skin and clothes.

Only about one in four people still smoke, so nonsmokers are a clear majority. Yet, because of the great danger in secondhand smoke, nonsmokers must also protect themselves.

Mold and Mildew: Age-old Toxins

Unlike many of the newer pollutants, mold and mildew have been with us since time immemorial, ever since water was allowed to stand over long period of time. In many sensitive or immuno-suppressed individuals, mold and mildew alone are a leading cause of environmental illness. Bronchial and sinus disorders as well as depression and chronic fatigue have been linked to mold sensitivity.

Wherever there is dampness or darkness, there is mold. Damp basements are a primary source of mold-producing spores that can spread throughout the house. Newspapers, magazines and books can easily accumulate mold as can old clothes, shoes, mattresses, carpeting and closets. The other predominant mold-producing areas of the house are the kitchen and bathroom. In the kitchen, mold can grow around leaky sinks and windows, in the surplus water tray on self-defrosting refrigerators and on the gasket of the refrigerator door. Mold can be found around the cold-water pipe and in the area between the sink and the wall. Wooden cooking utensils such as mixing spoons and cutting boards can accumulate mold as well as other bacteria. In the bathroom, molds can be found in the tile grouting around the sink, tub and walls. According to University of Oklahoma researchers, toothbrushes that are kept in humid bathrooms may be carriers of bacteria and viruses. Lined shower curtains can harbor mold.

Overwatered houseplants anywhere in the house can also be mold producers. Many times people mistakenly think they are al-lergic to some kind of foliage in the house when in fact they are reacting to the excess water on the soil surface of a houseplant. Mold spores can also enter the house from the plants outside. Grass, weeds and leaves right near the doors and windows can be additional mold sources.

Household Chemicals: A Constant Threat

Household products are everywhere: cleaners; disinfectants; detergents; aerosol sprays; oven cleaners; drain openers; carpet, rug and upholstery cleaners; toilet cleaners; room fresheners; furniture and floor polishes; spot removers; moth balls; lawn and garden chemicals; pest controls; paint and paint thinners and arts and crafts materials. In addition, consider the numbers of industrial chemicals that are illegally dumped in landfills which end up as sites for housing developments. These chemicals are still in the soil and can seep into your house.

Most people do not realize the amounts of poisons that can be found in everyday, seemingly tame household products. Oven cleaners and drain openers, for example, contain sodium hydroxide or lye which is extremely harmful when it is inhaled. Lye can burn through anything it touches. Floor and furniture polishes as well as spot removers, grease cutters and even rug cleaners contain powerful solvents. Liver and kidney damage, lung problems and nervous system disorders have been connected to solvent use. Aerosol sprays can hasten the introduction of poisons right into the body. The fine mist spray ensures easy inhalation and quick absorption to the respiratory system of concentrated toxins. As we have tightened our homes to save energy, we have unwittingly restricted proper air circulation which in turn has increased prolonged exposure to toxicity.

There are 50,000 pesticides available on the market, many of which are responsible for severe health problems. Perhaps the most toxic is chlordane, the chemical that was used for termite control. Chlordane remains toxic for up to 20 years. It can seep into 80 percent of the treated home, even when applied underground outside the home. It has been linked to neurologic disorders, miscarriages and cancers. Luckily, it was taken off the market in 1987, although exterminators can still legally use what is left in their reserves.

Paints, like pesticides, can also contain unhealthy chemicals. Lead, mercury and cadmium are often present in household paints. Lead affects the nervous and skeletal system, and can lead to severe learning disabilities and memory loss. Small children are at greater risk because they are likely to eat paint scrapings. Mercury, sometimes used as a fungicide in water-based paints, is a poison to the brain. Cadmium, found in yellow and orange colors, is associated with high blood pressure and kidney malfunction.

The short-term effects of household chemical exposure can include flulike symptoms, headaches, blurred vision, insomnia, irritability, depression, disorientation, heart palpitations, chronic colds and infections. Long-term effects may result in liver, kidney or lung damage, paralysis, diminished libido, sexual dysfunction and immunosuppression.

Carpets, Rugs and Furnishings: Sources of Unsuspected but Devastating Toxins

When a former patient and I moved into a magnificent home in the San Francisco Bay area, in a private wooded neighborhood with a gorgeous view, we had expectations of health and tranquility for research and writing. Soon after we settled down, however, we both began to sneeze and cough and then feel nauseous and fatigued. Conventional medical testing confirmed that these symptoms were not linked to diet, stress or allergy. It was only after we took an in-depth blood analysis at an environmental medicine clinic that we discovered the real cause of our symptoms—the brand-new synthetic wall-to-wall carpet that had been installed just before we moved in.

Even government regulatory agencies are not immune to the problems they are supposed to solve. "Sick Building Syndrome" hit the Environmental Protection Agency itself in Washington several years ago. Specialists found that it wasn't formaldehyde or asbestos or mold or even carbon monoxide that was creating the headaches, burning eyes, dizziness and other complaints affecting a sizable number of the agency's employees. It was the wall-to-wall synthetic carpeting. Apparently, a chemical called PC-4 produced by the latex backing of the carpet was the culprit. When dirt repellents, adhesives or rubber-based paddings are used in carpets, they are additional sources of toxic chemicals

Carpeting is a surprisingly toxic source of indoor pollution. Carpets are heavily sprayed with insecticides. They can harbor molds, mites, house dust and noxious odors. Even so-called natural wool carpets can be toxic because they may be mothproofed with chemicals. Toxic carpets are clearly one of the most lethal indoor polluters because there is chemical exposure all day and all night. Most other chemical exposure in the home or office is for a more limited period. Furniture and interior furnishings are another possible area of chemical contamination. Much of the wood furniture manufactured today is made of particle board, which creates outgassing from glue and formaldehyde over a long period of time. Also, sofas and upholstered chairs are filled with foam, polyester and polyurethane, all of which outgas toxic chemicals.

What You Can Do to Purify Your Indoor Environment

- Open windows, install exhaust fans, and install appliance vents that exhaust to the outside, especially if you are using a gas stove, water heater or clothes dryer.

- Vacuum rather than dust-mop or sweep floors with a broom. Dust and dirt particles can be scattered into the air, thus more easily inhaled. Water-based vacuum cleaners are excellent. Central vacuum cleaning systems also clean without creating dust.

- Drain and clean humidifiers weekly and clean air-conditioning filters frequently.

- The C.A.R.E. 2000 air purification system offers new breakthrough technology not previously available in residential air filtration systems. High-efficiency carbon and HEPA technology with superior air exchange and germicidal ultraviolet can eliminate bacteria and viruses. The system removes pollen, fumes, odors, particulates, formaldehyde, gases and smoke in addition to bacteria and viruses. Call Clean Water Revival for further information (see Resources).

- Change pet litter boxes daily. They are a great source of mold and harbor other problems such as parasites.

- Common household plants such as spider plants, elephant ear philodendron, Boston ferns, English ivy and aloe vera have been found by former NASA scientist Bill Wolverton, Ph.D. to be effective in removing a wide variety of indoor air pollutants. For example, aloe vera was discovered to be 90 percent effective in eliminating formaldehyde fumes in low concentrations. As Wolverton states in the December 1997 *Townsend Letter for Doctors and Patients:*

To the human eye, plants may appear static and nonreactive as they continue their normal process of living and growing. But in scientific terms, plants are highly dynamic, actively creating and emitting a cloud of complex, invisible substances around their leaves and roots that provide for their protection and well being. Houseplants do more than enhance the appearance of our surroundings: they can play an integral role in improving the very essence of our lives—the air we breathe.

Radon Solutions

Because radon is an odorless, colorless gas, we cannot detect it with our senses. Nor can we rely on test results our neighbors have received, since two similar houses close to one another can have very different radon levels. Several low-cost monitors to measure radon levels in the home are available. They include a charcoal canister monitor that uses a three- to seven-day measurement and an alpha-track detector that uses a two- to four-week measurement. Using the alpha-track detector for a full year provides the most reliable measurement. The monitor should be placed at the house's lowest level, usually the basement, where radon levels are likely to be highest. The highest acceptable radon level within a home, set by the EPA, is 4 picocuries per liter of air. When people receive an unfavorable measurement, there are some things they can do that require relatively little expense or effort to correct the problem.

- Open all windows regularly to provide cross ventilation. Replacing the air from time to time is a refreshing and healthy thing to do anyway, even if there is no radon problem.

- Set up a fan to draw air from the space between the basement floor and the foundation. The EPA claims that doing this can lower the radon level by 90 percent.

- Keep all basement ventilation ducts and vents open all year round.

- Because cement block walls are very porous to radon gas, seal their interiors with latex paint or topcoat.

- Seal cracks in the basement floor and subsurface walls.

- Face the interior of subsurface basement walls with particle board or Masonite to cut down radon seepage into a house.

- For new construction, install pipes allowing the radon to filter from the soil under the foundation. Pipes should be connected to an outside fan which draws radon away from the house. Line the foundation with plastic, making sure all holes around the pipes are completely sealed. In older buildings, seal all cracks and openings in the basement or around pumps and pipes with caulking and epoxy.

- Install a fan or ion generator to increase ventilation: the fan circulates the radioactive particles while the ion generator makes the particles harmlessly stick on the wall. Negative ion generators (also helpful to weather-sensitive individuals) change the electrical charge of oxygen molecules from positive to negative. Positive ions are generated from air conditioning, heating and smoking. Studies show that negative ions improve energy, health and moods. Positive ions slow down oxygen delivery whereas negative ions increase it.

- Don't smoke or allow smoking in your home. Tobacco smoke acts as a carrier of radon right to the smoker's and non-smoker's lungs, making them more susceptible to lung cancer.

- Filter all water for all possible radon contamination. The initial screening tests for radon are relatively inexpensive.

- For more information, call the Environmental Protection Agency (see Resources).

Formaldehyde Solutions

- Houseplants to the rescue. Remember that according to former NASA research scientist Bill Wolverton, there are many plants that can reduce the levels of many pollutants, including formaldehyde. As Dr. Wolverton states, "About 15 to 20 plants should completely remove formaldehyde from an 1800 square foot house."

- For new home builders, use whole wood products or formaldehyde-free wood boards and adhesives instead of pressed wood materials like plywood, fiber board and particle board. Particle board is manufactured by gluing wood chips together with urea formaldehyde resin. This resin constitutes as much as ten percent of the finished weight of the particle board.

- Avoid urea formaldehyde foam insulation.

- Be aware that new furniture, drapes and carpeting are additional sources of formaldehyde.

- Open windows daily when these products are new.

- Avoid excess heat and humidity in your home if you suspect there are formaldehyde fumes. By keeping the indoor temperature 10 degrees less than normal, you can reduce formaldehyde outgassing by up to 50 percent.

- If you cannot replace the particle board, apply a polyurethane sealer to reduce formaldehyde outgassing.

Carbon Monoxide Solutions

- Before the cold weather begins, when you will be spending more time in the house, have your local gas company check for leaks. Periodic safety checks on your gas stove, heater and furnace exhaust system are a good prevention measure.

- Open windows, especially in the kitchen. Use a hood fan or some kind of exhaust fan that vents outside for gas or wood cooking.

- Make sure water-heating gas furnaces and clothes dryers are vented to the outside.

- Check burner flames for a blue color at the tips of the flame; yellow or orange-tipped flames signify a high level of carbon monoxide (up to 30 times the normal level). Alert the gas company immediately.

- Convert the pilot light in gas stoves to an electric spark ignition. Pilot lights use up to 30 percent of the gas and emit constant amounts of pollutants.

- Use kerosene space heaters only in rooms with good cross-ventilation.

- Warm up the car outside, not in the garage, especially if the garage is closed or attached to the house.

Mildew Solutions

- Throw out old reading material and clothing stored in damp places.

- Air out or clean mattresses, carpeting and closets.

- Install a dehumidifier in any room which is excessively damp, primarily the basement.

- Keep all wet surfaces and towels dry, particularly in the basement, kitchen and bathroom.

- Sprinkle Borax, which has natural antimold properties, over any area which has mold.

- Change your toothbrush frequently, especially after you've recovered from a cold or the flu.

- Eliminate mold growing on the surface soil of household plants by placing crushed stones on the soil surface.

- Keep grass, weeds and leaves away from windows and the entrance to the house.

Smoking Solutions

- If you are a smoker, stop!

- Nonsmokers should use their majority status to achieve the following goals. Many of these suggestions are offered by the American Lung Association:

—Educate your children at home and at school to understand that cigarettes and smoking are pollutants and a poison dangerous to those that smoke and to those that do not.

—Support legislation to restrict smoking or to set up restricted smoking areas in public places.

—Ask doctors, dentists, health care professionals and hospital staff to restrict smoking in waiting areas or establish no-smoking regulations.

—Encourage restaurants to establish no-smoking areas.

—Propose no-smoking resolutions at club and organization meetings.

—Request no-smoking sections when you travel.

—Put up no-smoking signs in your home, office or car.

—Tell friends, family, coworkers and strangers that you *do* mind if they smoke.

—Protest the glorification of smoking in films and television.

—Use an ion generator, or better yet, one with an air purifier, to clear smoke-filled rooms.

Household Chemical Solutions

• Increasing the number of decorative household plants is one way to absorb toxic chemicals in the home.

• Ventilate, ventilate, ventilate. Opening windows for at least 15 minutes a day is very helpful to recirculate good air.

• A new cleaning cloth called Envirocloth can help you clean more effectively without harmful chemicals. This innovative cloth, which lasts an average of two to three years, has extremely fine fibers that trap and emulsify grease and dirt using only water. Envirocloth can remove grease from glass, difficult stains from carpets and perform other tough cleaning jobs. Envirocloth has been used in millions of European households since 1985. For further information call 1-800-487-0630.

- Try to buy products that are biodegradable, nontoxic and low-phosphate. You might consider using Borax, vinegar and baking soda as a basis for all your cleaning and disinfectant needs.

- Use fresh fragrant flowers and baking soda for room fresheners. Simmer herbs and spices for natural fragrances.

- Use water-based paints without petrochemicals and paint thinners made from plant oils.

- Use water-based markers, paints and materials for arts and crafts supplies.

- To avoid termites, keep all firewood at least 30 feet from the house.

- Investigate the noncarcinogenic termite control products called *permethrins* to replace toxic termidicides if you have termite infestation.

- Open windows when painting indoors and use a fan for optimal air circulation. For outdoor painting, select a wind-free and dry day to paint.

Carpets, Rugs and Furnishing Solutions

- If possible, avoid installing wall-to-wall synthetic carpeting.

- If you live in a house with wall-to-wall carpeting that was installed a year or more ago, it has probably outgassed and will emit no more toxic fumes.

- If you are in a brand-new home with new wall-to-wall carpeting or building a home, you can consider replacing the carpeting and rugs with glazed or stone-based tile like terrazzo or quarry tile. If you want to keep the carpet, leave all your windows open for at least a month so that ventilation can clear away the toxins.

- Unfortunately, even wool carpeting is suspect, since it is very hard to find wool carpet that is not mothproofed with pesticides.

- If you must install synthetic carpeting, check the major specs regarding the chemicals used in the carpeting and choose the least toxic carpet. Look for Carpet and Rug Institute (CRI) low-emission labels before buying. Allow any synthetic carpeting you plan to install to air outside for several days before you install it.

- Many synthetic carpets have been found to outgas a number of tongue-twisting chemicals. Try to select more natural materials for your floor coverings such as cotton area rugs.

- The following room-by-room checklist will enable you to get an idea of how many potential sources of pollution exist in your own home. But keep in mind that one strong source, such as a new carpet, may be far more harmful than ten less toxic ones.

Bedroom

Wall-to-wall carpeting	Electric blanket
Vinyl or fabric wallpaper	Kerosene space heater
Drapes	Humidifier

Mothballs

Digital clock

Permanent-press sheets

Synthetic mattress (dust and mites)

Particle board bedroom set

Television

Recently dry-cleaned clothes in closet

Bathroom

Aerosol personal care products

Room deodorizer

Cosmetics

Perfumes

Personal deodorant containing aluminum

Scented or colored toilet paper

Toilet disinfectant or deodorant

Moldy shower stall or curtain

Worn toothbrushes

Mold around tiles and pipes

Kitchen

Aluminum cookware

Liquid floor wax

Unvented gas stove

Fluorescent lights

Microwave oven

Cleaners and disinfectants

Aerosol sprays

Mold under sinks or in refrigerator

Pressed-wood cabinets

Radioactive smoke detector

Unfiltered tap water

Attached garage

Living Room

Radioactive smoke detector

Synthetic wall-to-wall carpeting

Liquid floor wax

Fireplace or wood stove

Radioactive smoke alarm

Particle board wall panels

Pressed- or softwood furniture or floor

Overwatered potted plants with moldy soil

Air conditioner

Cigarette smoke

Laundry Room

Unvented gas or electric dryer

Bleaches

Scented detergents

Fabric softeners

Chlorinated scouring powders

Portable vacuum cleaner

Polishes

Dusters, mops, brooms

Gas water heater with asbestos lining

Home Office

Personal computer

Copy machine

Plastic, laminated or veneered furniture

Plastic boxes, files, bins

Electric typewriter

Marking pens

Typing correction fluid

Garage

Attached to house

Gas furnace

Gas heating and cooling system

Chemical pesticides and fertilizers

Moldy books or newspapers

Stored clothing and shoes

General Structure

Urea formaldehyde or asbestos insulation

Slab floor

Unshielded electrical cable

Vapor barrier

Radon

Home near microwave tower or airport

Home near toxic waste dump

Home near power cables of substation

Lifestyle Habits

Family members who smoke

Arts and crafts or hobby supplies

8

Detoxifying Your Indoor Light Environment

Light is essential to life, yet also a potential danger to our health. It can keep us young and vital or make us tired and depressed. The understanding of how light affects our health and emotional well-being has progressed in leaps and bounds over the past two decades. As Dr. John Ott, pioneering researcher on the effects of light on health, has said, "Light is a nutrient much like food. The wrong kind can make us ill and the right kind can make us well." Our bodies use light very much like water or food in a variety of metabolic processes. The light entering the retina of the eyes influences the master glands—the pituitary, hypothalamus and pineal glands—which control the entire endocrine system.

For the last 50 years, in books such as *Health and Light* and *Light, Radiation and You,* Dr. Ott has been warning against the unhealthy effects of artificial fluorescent lights as well as wearing sunglasses outdoors, which are robbing us of adequate exposure to the therapeutic effects of the full-spectrum light. (One important caution: some researchers suggest that sunglasses may be helpful in preventing macular degeneration in blue-eyed people.) Light expert Dr. George Brainard of Thomas Jefferson Medical School in Philadelphia believes that artificial lighting indoors is "grossly inadequate for our biological requirements."

The only healthful artificial light is full-spectrum light which is composed of the entire range of frequencies of natural sunlight. Luckily, full-spectrum lighting, which most closely approximates natural sunlight, is now available on the market. The advantages of full-spectrum lighting over regular incandescent and fluorescent lighting include improved vision, hormone regulation, reduced PMS symptoms, and enhanced absorption of vitamin D and calcium, as well as reduced stress, depression, hyperactivity and fatigue. Sufficient natural light is particularly important because solar radiation activates important biochemical activities in our bodies. Natural light is responsible for the timing of our biological clocks, our 24-hour circadian rhythms, which regulate our wakefulness, mood, appetite, and much of our immunologic response.

Sunlight is the only form of natural, healthy light. Yet, we often block the sun's healthful rays from getting to our retina by wearing sunglasses. Even regular glasses and contact lenses block some of the essential rays we need.

According to Dr. Ott, the most damaging category of artificial light are the gaseous discharged types of light such as mercury vapor, sodium vapor and limited-spectrum fluorescent light. These emit radiation that grossly weakens muscle strength and thus affects behavior and academic achievement. Dr. Ott has found that both teachers and pupils had frequent complaints of headaches, eyestrain and other health-related problems in classrooms and schools where gas-discharge types of lights were used.

Seasonal Affective Disorder (SAD)

Scientists now know that the deprivation of full-spectrum light is the cause of a modern illness called Seasonal Affective Disorder (SAD), a form of depression caused by a lack of natural light as the days grow shorter in late fall when light levels are low and we spend more time indoors. Nearly 12 million people may be suffering from SAD in the United States. The best definition I have ever read of this disorder comes from a wonderful book called *Light Years Ahead,* edited by Brian Breiling, Ph.D. and Bethany ArgIsle.

SAD is a severe depressive illness that regularly manifests in late fall (precipitated by light deprivation) and subsides with the longer, sunnier days of spring. The severity and incidence of SAD symptoms increase the farther away from the equator's longer and brighter days. Anyone deprived of regular sunlight exposure can suffer from SAD.

Symptoms are similar to other forms of depressive illness: lethargy, fatigue, decreased energy and activity level, anxiety, irritability, lowered sex drive, avoidance of social activities, sadness and depressed mood, concentration difficulties, interpersonal difficulties. SAD symptoms differ from other depressive illnesses in the time of year of onset and the sufferer's unusually intense desire for sleep (sometimes beyond 16 hours a day), craving for sweets and carbohydrates (especially in the late afternoon and evening) and increased appetite and weight gain.

Scientists speculate that these symptoms may be due to an increased production of the hormone melatonin (melatonin has a sedative effect on the body, and the body releases more melatonin at night). Winter's long nights lead to increased melatonin production and an even greater sedative effect.

Another theory is that SAD may be related to a decreased concentration of serotonin, the neurotransmitter that regulates the stress response. It is artificially increased by certain antidepressants such as Prozac. Light is really a natural Prozac because it increases our serotonin levels naturally.

Dr. Norman Rosenthal, M.D., of the National Institute of Mental Health, has significantly contributed to our understanding of the cause and cure of SAD. Dr. Rosenthal has pioneered an effective treatment for those who have depression caused by deprivation of full-spectrum light. He prescribes spending one-half to three (and sometimes more) hours daily within one to two feet of a special light box which contains full-spectrum light.

Dr. Rosenthal reports that most winter depression symptoms subside after using the light for at least one week. However, depression will return if the patient is again deprived of full-spectrum light for just a few days. Approximately 80 percent of SAD patients improve within one week of full-spectrum light therapy. Light is also being used for nonseasonal depression, eating disorders and a host of psychiatric conditions Light can even help patients' responses to medication, especially in those who were previously unresponsive.

There is now a new device available for SAD sufferers called the Brio-Brite Light Visor, which is worn on the head. It was developed by a research team of scientists from the National Institute of Mental Health and the Thomas Jefferson Medical Center.

For those who have difficulty getting up during winter's dark mornings and want to hibernate, a special computerized light alarm clock, called a dawn simulator, will awaken them gently to increasing levels of brightness. Even a small amount of incandescent light in a bedside lamp effectively suppresses quality sleep. The dawn simulator allows one to awaken gradually refreshed, alert and ready to greet the day.

Full-spectrum Fluorescent Lights

John Ott created the first full-spectrum bulbs called the Ott-Lite Full Spectrum. Another company, called Duro-Test Corporation in Fairfield, New Jersey, is the manufacturer of one of the most widely used full-spectrum fluorescent light tubes, called Vita-Light. Duro-Test's researchers believe that the last two or three generations are the first to have spent nearly three-quarters of their lives under artificial light, and don't yet know its effect on health. They recognize sunlight, along with food, air and water, as the most important survival factors in human life.

Vita-Light is a patented, general-purpose fluorescent tube that simulates the full color and ultraviolet spectrum of sunlight. Because Vita-Light reveals detail and color accurately, people see better under Vita-Light, according to Duro-Test's research. Vita-Lights come in standard fluorescent tube lengths and can replace the fluorescent tube in standard fixtures. Although they initially cost more than regular fluorescent tubes, they are in fact a good buy since they last up to 24,000 hours. Many clinical studies have shown that Vita-Lights are beneficial to plants as well because they provide the benefits of natural outdoor light and enhance germination, flowering and general growth. They are also ideal for pets and aquariums, because they provide a natural light environment.

Light Giveth and Light Taketh Away

In addition to assisting with SAD, light can be used as a healing modality for an enormous variety of maladies ranging from allergies to immune disorders. In *Light Years Ahead,* 12 cutting edge clinicians (including Dr. John Downing, my former light therapist and inventor of the Lumatron Ocular Light Stimulator) discuss the connection between light therapy and mind/body healing. The book describes the latest therapeutic uses of light in medicine, optometry, chiropractic, acupuncture, education and psychotherapy. It explains how visible light taken in through the eyes or absorbed by the body can be used to improve mood, sleep, intellectual and visual performance, as well as aid in recovery from jet lag and promote general well-being. The book also includes documented case histories that successfully demonstrate the dramatic effect of light applied to a wide variety of maladies including major depression, SAD, PMS, chronic fatigue, allergies, immune disorders, learning difficulties, visual and neurological problems, and recovery from physical, sexual and emotional abuse. Many of the recommendations contained in the following section have been adapted from *Light Years Ahead*.

What You Can Do to Enhance Your Environment with Light

- Spend at least 20 minutes a day outside to allow the sun's full-spectrum light to enter your pupils.

- If you wear sunglasses while you're outside, remove the glasses for small periods of time to allow the sun to enter your eyes.

- Replace all gaseous discharge types of light (mercury vapor, sodium vapor and limited-spectrum fluorescent lights) with full-spectrum fluorescent lights—especially in kitchen areas, shop areas or any area where one spends any length of time in specialized tasks or reading. There are full-spectrum lightbulbs now for recessed ceiling lights.

- Supplement your light diet. Replace all yellowish-appearing incandescent bulbs in your home with full-spectrum fluorescents that screw into the incandescent sockets. Such products as the Ott-Lite capsulite bulb are now available for this purpose.

- Humans have a minimum daily requirement for sunlight of between one-half to two hours a day. There is never a need to risk sunburn, since the requisite brightness can be attained on cloudy days or under the shade of a tree. But, UV rays are still present, so be careful.

- See Resources for a list of companies who carry a variety of full-spectrum lights for home, office or personal use.

9
Detoxifying Your Water

I remember reading an article many years ago in *Good House-keeping* magazine which stated, "Every time you turn on your faucet, you are committing an act of faith. You believe that the water you give your child to drink, the water with which you cook and wash your food, is fit for human use. Don't take it for granted." Such prophetic words really ring true today as we read, almost on a daily basis, about how contaminated our water supply is by chemicals, toxins, radioactive residues and parasites. Just pick up any newspaper or magazine. The headlines speak for themselves.

> More than 1 in 5 Americans unknowingly drink tap water polluted with feces, radiation or other contaminants. . . . Nearly 1,000 deaths each year and at least 400,000 cases of waterborne illness may be attributed to contaminated water . . . (*The New York Times,* June 2, 1995)
>
> Parasites in water are widespread. . . . can be dangerous, even fatal, to people with weakened immune systems. (*USA Today,* March 30, 1995)

Nearly 80 percent of the composition of the average adult body consists of water. As little as a 15 percent loss of water will cause death. Water is the key to body functions including temperature control, digestion, elimination, assimilation and circulatory systems. To give you an idea of just how vital water is for survival, consider this: man can live for five weeks without food but only five days without water. The World Health Organization states that 80 percent of world illnesses would be eliminated by drinking pure water. The problem is where to find it.

Pure water has become extinct. In this day and age one cannot assume that water is pollutant-free regardless of the source. Just because it comes out of your kitchen faucet is no guarantee for purity. This is also true for spring and well water. Newspapers and television newscasts report almost daily how water pollution is increasing from the sewage and industrial waste being dumped directly into our water resources.

While we are becoming aware that our drinking water is contaminated by the deluge of pesticides plus agricultural and industrial run-off, we are also beginning to realize the extent of water contamination from chemical dumps as well as buried oil or gas tanks and lines. These chemicals soak into the soil and into the earth's underground water reservoirs. Even those individuals who get their drinking water from wells and springs run a risk of drinking chemical- and bacteria-ridden water. A whole variety of pollutants is being found in wells all over the country. Giardia and cryptosporidium as well as other waterborne parasites have been found in over 90 percent of surface water across the United States alone. Globally, thousands die every day from disease-causing microbes in drinking water.

Although most of the earth's water is unfit for human consumption, modern technology has provided a positive solution. Water is more easily purified than food or air because of point-of-use water filtration. The water in our reservoirs, wells and springs may be unfit for human consumption, yet we can easily purify contaminated water through point-of-use water filtration in our homes and businesses.

Point-of-use filtration has the potential to virtually empower all of us to provide ourselves with pure water. Remember, most municipal water treatment plants do not supply pure water nor is well or spring water necessarily pure.

Let's look at some of the pollutants in our water. Water has become severely contaminated by chemicals and toxins. Every year over 18 billion pounds of pollutants and chemicals are released by industry into the atmosphere, soil and groundwater. Over 70,000 chemical compounds are now in use by industry, agriculture and individual citizens, with 5,000 new chemical compounds being introduced every year. At least 700 of these chemicals have been identified in America's drinking water. Safety limits have been set for little over 100 of these chemicals. The harmful chemicals and metals that are present cannot necessarily be seen, tasted or smelled. One of the most hazardous chemicals to our health is actually added to our water supplies by water treatment plants. This chemical is chlorine.

The Chlorine Connection

Chlorine is a major toxic chemical in drinking water. Used as a disinfectant against bacteria, it is ineffective against parasites such as giardia and cryptosporidium. Chlorine has been linked to heart disease and cancer. Even those who don't drink chlorinated water often swim, shower or bathe in it. Because the skin is not a barrier to chemicals in the water like chlorine, we can still absorb the chlorine into our bodies.

Poisonous chlorine gas used in Europe during World War I was responsible for the deaths of hundreds of thousands of people, thus the western Europeans do not use chlorine to purify their water. Instead they use ozone and ultraviolet light. We may be heading in the same direction as research continues to prove how unhealthy chlorinated water may be. Dr. Joseph Price, M.D., from Saginaw General Hospital in Michigan, states, "Chlorine is the greatest crippler and killer of modern times; it is an insidious poison . . . We thought we were preventing epidemics of one disease, but we were creating another." In 1987, the *Journal of the National Cancer Institute* reported that chlorinated water is the cause of 12 percent of bladder cancer cases. This percentage rises to 27 percent among smokers.

Chlorine reacts with water's natural organic matter, creating new carcinogenic compounds called trihalomethanes or THMs. The most well-known and best researched of the THMs is chloroform. Chloroform is a solvent and a general anesthetic. It is the stuff used to knock people out. It can cause kidney, liver and nervous system damage, and has been associated with cancer in laboratory experiments. If there is chlorine in your water, you are being sprayed with chloroform every time you take a shower. Emissions from hot showers can dissolve 50 percent of the chlorine and 80 percent of other carcinogens, like tetrachlorethylene and radon in the water. You are then breathing and soaking in these chemicals through your skin. (Please note, however, that Clorox bleach, which I will be recommending in the next chapter as a cleansing bath to detoxify food, is not the same as chlorine. Clorox breaks down into salt and water.) Drinking contaminated water is not the only way water becomes dangerous to your health. One-half of all water pollution exposure is through the skin and lungs via hot showers and baths.

In his newsletter *Health and Healing,* Dr. Julian Whitaker says that in early July of 1997, the public health commissioner of Washington, D.C. issued a warning to parents of infants, the elderly and people with immune system problems to boil tap water before drinking it. A few days later, this was followed by the announcement that 60 percent more chlorine would be added to city water. Residents were told this super-chlorinated water was "okay" to drink, but were warned not to add it to aquariums because it would kill the fish.

While granting that chlorination is effective against many but not all bacteria in water, experts increasingly question the wisdom of trading the risk of bacterial infection for the risk of bladder cancer. Some strongly advise against all chlorination of drinking water. Others suggest a change in its technology, including increased use of granular-activated charcoal and the use of ozone gas. In addition, it has been suggested that chlorination be the last rather than the initial step of water treatment to reduce the amount of trihalomethanes.

The Sweet Poison

Lead is possibly one of the most dangerous pollutants found in drinking water today. Health researchers fear that one out of five Americans (about 38 million) is exposed to dangerously high levels of lead in drinking water. As previously mentioned, lead is responsible for kidney, brain and nervous system disorders. It can cause hypertension in adults and has been connected to multiple sclerosis and impotency. Children under nine are particularly vulnerable to lead exposure which can stunt their growth and cause learning disabilities. High levels of lead have been noted in children experiencing lethargy, personality aberrations and mental retardation. High levels of lead can cause miscarriages, nerve damage in fetuses and even death.

Today, private and municipal companies are required by law to test for lead. However, they test only where water is stored. Lead leaches into drinking water through lead pipes to your home or lead solder that connects the household plumbing. A federal ban against using lead in plumbing systems took effect in June 1988. The problem still remains in those homes where lead was used before the ban.

Fluoride

Fluoride, the substance said to strengthen tooth enamel, is another savior-turned-disabler which is added to our water as a dental aid. Ironically, while it may strengthen tooth enamel, it can also cause permanent mottling of the teeth as well as more serious maladies. Fluoride is known to weaken the immune system and cause heart disease, birth defects and genetic damage. Fluoride is a potent factor in aging. Dr. John Yiamouyiannis, the foremost world authority on fluoride's biological effects, claims that fluoride is responsible for the chronic poisoning of over 130,000,000 Americans. Yiamouyiannis' research also reveals that fluoride is a potent contributor to allergy, arthritis and cancer. But the good news is that, like chlorine, fluoride should and can be removed through special point-of-use water filtration.

Iron

As previously discussed, excess iron can be particularly dangerous for those individuals suffering from hemachromatosis or genetic iron overload, a condition that can lead to heart disease and arthritis. Excessive iron in water can cause a metallic taste, stain fixtures and clog plumbing pipes. Well water containing iron can look clear when you drink it, but prolonged exposure to air will oxidize the iron in the water which eventually becomes cloudy with a red sediment that settles in the bottom of the glass. Water that contains an excessive amount of manganese shows the same qualities except that manganese shows up as dark brown sediment.

Other Toxins in Water

Polluted water contains nitrates. Even low concentrations of nitrogen have caused illness in infants and occasionally death. Nitrates take the oxygen out of the water and cause a decreased ability to carry oxygen in the blood. It can be the cause of a condition in babies called "Blue Baby." Hydrogen sulfide, a gas found in water, can give off a foul, rotten-egglike odor. It is unpleasant to smell and drink. Sulfates also can make the water unpleasant to drink. They impart a medicinal taste and can have a laxative effect. Barium, selenium, cadmium, chromium, silver, zinc and copper, along with lead and manganese, have designated maximum contaminant levels set by the 1974 Federal Safe Drinking Water Act.

Total Dissolved Solids (TDS) refers to the sum total of all mineral compounds dissolved in the drinking water. Excessive TDSs can cause health problems as well as water-use problems such as ineffective cleaning capabilities.

Parasites

Even if well water is not contaminated by industrial seepage, pesticides or waste materials there is a good chance it is contaminated by parasites. There have been outbreaks of *Giardia lamblia,* a waterborne protozoan, in nearly every state in America. Giardia, as discussed in Chapter 4, is a parasite carried by all domestic animals that comes into the water system when these animals deposit their waste in or near water sources. Symptoms such as diarrhea, nausea, weight loss and alternating constipation and diarrhea have all been connected to giardia. Outbreaks have been particularly noted in mountainous areas where the water supply is thought to be more pristine and free from contamination. The parasite cryptosporidium was responsible for the largest outbreak of waterborne disease in United States history. In 1993, over 400,000 people became ill, and over 100 died in Milwaukee as a result of a cryptosporidium outbreak in the municipal water system. More than ten other outbreaks have occurred in our country in the past ten years.

Hard vs. Soft

It is easy to understand that chemicals, bacteria and parasites in drinking water can cause health problems, but only recently have we discovered that the regular consumption of hard or highly mineralized water can actually benefit health. Water hardness is caused by the presence of either calcium or magnesium compounds in the water. It is now recognized by leading researchers that a high magnesium level in water can reduce heart disease risk, particularly among men. On the other hand, a high calcium content in the water supply often creates a deficiency in magnesium, zinc and potassium.

Water hardness is measured in grains. In order that water look and taste good as well as perform other cleaning functions that prevent it from stiffening laundry or clogging pipes, water hardness should not exceed four grains per gallon. The traditional water hardness scale starts at three grains and goes to ten grains, which is considered very hard.

Another important factor in the measurement of water is pH balance. PH balance measures the relative acidity and/or alkalinity of the water. PH is measured on a scale of 0–14; 0–7 is acid, 7.0 is neutral, and 7–14 is alkaline. The harder the water, the more likely it is alkaline. Naturally soft water, such as rain water, is acidic. PH readings below 7 mean the water can cause damage to pipes and equipment by corrosion. A reading above 7 will cause scaling and clogging of plumbing. It is best to have a pH water reading of 6.5–8.5. This water pH can be achieved through proper water softening, using a magnetic conditioning system.

Bottled Water to the Rescue?

The onslaught of information concerning water contamination has been a boon to bottled water sales. On the face of it, one would assume that bottled water is a simple solution to the problem. However, in some cases bottled water may not be much better than tap water. So called "purified" water can actually be purified tap water. Surveys have revealed the widespread presence of various contaminants like bacteria and heavy metals in so-called purified water. Several companies have been indicted for marketing ordinary tap water as spring water. One study performed by the New York State Department of Health in 1987 reported that more than 50 percent of the bottled waters tested contained chemical contamination, in some cases exceeding the allowable levels for tap water.

There are many reputable bottled water products available nationwide. However, just because water is bottled and called spring water is no guarantee of its quality. Furthermore, if your bottled water is in plastic containers, plastic toxins can leach into the water—introducing another toxic poison. Domestic sources of bottled water do not come under as stringent regulations as imported water.

Some people think that distilled water is the safest of all water to drink. However, some studies indicate just the opposite. Dr. William Rea, who heads the Environmental Unit in Dallas, Texas, has found that distilled water is often the most contaminated of all bottled water. The process of distillation can vaporize and concentrate certain chemicals like chloroform. Distilling also removes essential trace minerals that are necessary for healthy body metabolism. For distilled water to be safe to drink, it must go through a double distillation process, something which most bottled water companies do not do.

How to Assure Your Water Is Pure

So, how can we acquire pure water? I have devoted several years of research to answer this question. All of my research suggests that the ultimate solution to the elimination of all water contaminants—chemicals, heavy metals, bacteria, viruses and parasites—is a multistage ceramic-carbon filter with an ultraviolet attachment. If nitrates and heavy metals are high, an additional reverse osmosis system can be added on. If the water is hard due to calcium (rather than heart-protecting magnesium), a point-of-use water softening unit that does not, like traditional water softeners, add sodium, can be utilized.

The water-softening process works on an ion exchange principle, exchanging sodium ions for calcium or heavy metal ions. The older water-softening systems used more salt in the softening process, thus retaining more salt in the end product. Besides being harmful to us as drinking water, this softened water added to the salinity of the soil (a growing concern for environmentalists) as it drained back into the earth. The new generation of softeners or magnetic water conditioners are much more efficient because they give the best of both worlds—all of the beneficial minerals present in hard water along with many of the cleansing benefits softened water provides. Not all water conditioning companies use magnetic water conditioners. There are still many popular companies that are selling equipment that uses the older softening process, producing highly saline water that is unhealthy and undrinkable.

What are some of the benefits of using softened water? Softened water saves on gas and electric bills because it takes 29.57 percent more gas to produce hot water with hard water than with softened water. With electric water heating systems it takes 21–68 percent more energy to heat hard water as compared with softened water. Softened water requires less soap or cleaning compounds to do their job. Equipment such as clothes washers, dishwashers and hot water heaters have a prolonged life.

Softening performs yet another very important function: it removes larger molecules such as cadmium, arsenic and lead. However, we still need to remove smaller molecules such as chlorine and fluoride as well as bacteria, viruses and parasites. Ceramic-carbon with ultraviolet and reverse osmosis are the two main methods for accomplishing this. Ceramic filtration has been used worldwide for over 140 years and has been proven to be the best method to eliminate parasites from drinking water. The ceramic is "bacteriostatic" and does not allow bacteria to breed. With a special carbon core blended with a heavy metal compound, it eliminates dirt, chlorine, lead, bad taste, odor, pesticides and many other toxic substances. Adding an ultraviolet unit gives the added protection against bacteria and viruses. It can be installed on the faucet or under the sink and is compact and cost-effective.

Reverse osmosis (RO) is a process whereby water passes through a fine semipermeable membrane. The water first passes through a prefilter where suspended matter and undissolved solids are removed. The water is then forced through the extremely fine membrane. In this stage, pure water molecules are separated from the remaining dissolved solids and other contaminants. After this, the water enters a pressurized storage tank where it is stored until we tap into it. At the point where the water is brought from the storage tank there is an activated carbon post filter through which the water passes on the way to the tap. Only extremely small molecules can pass through the pores of the RO membrane; thus the membrane holds back large molecules such as bacteria, viruses and parasites. The carbon filter takes care of taste and odor.

What are the benefits of drinking RO water? Pure water acts as a chelating agent, that is, because it is devoid of chemical substances, minerals and metals it will naturally draw out any of these elements already stored in the body and help the body cleanse and detoxify. Water-stored elements always want to flow to the area of least concentration; therefore, the pure water acts as a magnet to the various elements. In short, drinking pure water does more than just keep toxins from our bodies; the water actually help clean our bodies internally. Pure water is a very powerful solvent for cleaning our houses and clothes as well.

There is, however, one major disadvantage in this chelating action of pure water: it will pull out important minerals as well as impurities. Therefore, it is important to take an ionic trace mineral supplement if you drink RO water.

What You Can Do to Purify Your Water

I recommend the Doulton Ceramic Water Filter, the most effective water filtration system available. The filter is made of ultrafine ceramic with pores so small that they trap bacteria, parasites and particles down to 0.5 microns in size. Unlike some other filter systems, the Doulton system does not create an environment for bacterial growth inside itself. The Doulton filtering method consists of three stages. In the first stage, the tiny pores in the ceramic remove bacteria, parasites, rust and dirt. The second filter stage is composed of high-density matrix carbon that removes chlorine, pesticides and other chemicals. In the third stage, a heavy metal-removing compound removes lead and copper.

One advantage of the Doulton filter over the water distillation method is time; it can take up to six hours to distill a gallon of water. An advantage over reverse osmosis is that the Doulton filter doesn't waste water, while reverse osmosis systems use three gallons to produce one gallon of drinkable water. The Doulton filter retains its maximum effectiveness for up to 1,100 gallons of water. On average, a family of four would need to change its Doulton filter only once a year. The ceramic cartridge can be removed at any time and given a light scrubbing.

If, however, nitrates or other heavy metals are present, a reverse osmosis system can be used in combination with a ceramic ultraviolet filter. For more information about or to order a Doulton, see Resources.

If your water is hard with calcium (not magnesium) deposits, you might also consider a magnetic water-conditioning system such as the GMX system. GMX International in Chico, California manufactures and distributes magnetic water-conditioning systems, a salt-free solution to treating hard water for residential and commercial applications. GMX magnetic fluid treatment accomplishes many of the same benefits of traditional salt-softening without the contaminating effluence produced by most salt softeners. GMX systems have been proven effective by both university testing and thousands of satisfied customers. GMX systems have a 100 percent satisfaction guarantee. For more information, see Resources. I use both the Doulton and GMX in my home in Montana.

If you prefer not to install a home filtration system, buy your water in glass bottles or ceramic containers, not plastic. If you cannot locate a brand such as Mountain Valley and want bottled water, ask various bottled water companies for a pesticide and mineral analysis. If you already subscribe to a bottled water service, ask the company for its water analysis information.

If you are still using tap water, use only the cold water for drinking and cooking. There is a greater probability that the hot water contains lead, asbestos and other pollutants. Let the cold water tap run for a few minutes until it is as cold as it can get to flush out the pipes. The longer water sits in the pipes, the higher the lead content.

10
Detoxifying Your Food

Food is so basic to good health that the latest frontier in disease prevention is the use of whole foods and whole-food concentrates because of the phytochemicals they contain. Phytochemicals are biologically active compounds found in a variety of colorful fruits and vegetables. Phytochemicals such as the carotenoids, beta-carotene, alpha-carotene, lycopene and xanthophylls, for example, show great potential for lowering cancer risk as well as boosting immune function. In fact, lycopene, a carotenoid found primarily in tomatoes, has been the focus of research as a protective agent against prostate cancer. There is additional evidence that shows the potential of phytochemicals in the reduction of tumors and cancerous cells; some stop potential cancer cells from even forming. They may also be able to enhance the immune system.

That's the good news. The bad news is that much of our food supply is not only tainted but is actually becoming hazardous to our health. This is due to a whole new variety of food invaders ranging from E. coli to irradiation to genetic engineering that is challenging our long-term health and well-being. It remains to be seen whether these new hidden dangers will neutralize the healing effects of phytochemicals.

To add further insult to injury, most commercial foods are laced with pesticides, herbicides and weed killers. Moreover, the *Seattle*

Times reported that toxic heavy metals, chemicals and radioactive wasters are being recycled as fertilizer and spread over farmers' fields nationwide. In Washington State, there is now a requirement that these elements be listed as ingredients. Hopefully, this protective requirement will be adopted throughout the United States.

These issues seem to make our ongoing concerns about the detrimental health effects of preservatives, additives and flavor enhancers rather insignificant when you consider that the bacteria *E. coli,* the latest addition to our food supply, can kill you. And food irradiation, the process the FDA has recommended to ensure food safety against *E. coli,* carries its own set of hazards.

E. Coli

During the past several years, national television, magazines and radio have alerted us to the newest health hazard lurking in our food. *E. coli,* a nasty bacteria that can be deadly, has now surfaced as the most serious health problem in food-borne illness. Carried in the intestines of animals, it enters the human system via undercooked beef. *E. coli* was the direct cause of four children's deaths back in 1993, and there may be as many as 20,000 infections a year in the United States that go unreported. Like parasite-based illness, the exact numbers of infected individuals may be much higher.

The symptoms of *E. coli* infection mimic other familiar diseases. This potential killer can cause bloody diarrhea and kidney failure. Although many individuals can survive *E. coli,* they can suffer a perforated colon and abdominal abscesses in the process, not to mention loss of lung function and the destruction of the lining of the heart. This deadly bacteria surfaced once again in the summer of 1997 when 25 million pounds of hamburger meat processed by Nebraska's Hudson Food Company were recalled due to *E. coli* contamination. This prompted the FDA to approve the irradiation of beef and other red meats like lamb, a process which the FDA believes will kill most bacteria like *E. coli* and salmonella in food. Irradiation has been used for many years on pork, poultry, spices and some fresh produce. These foods are identified with a special symbol, a flower contained within a circle, known as the radura symbol.

What Is Irradiation and How Safe Is It?

Dr. Gary Gibbs has written a must-read book about the dangers of food irradiation entitled *The Food That Would Last Forever.* Since the FDA has now approved beef irradiation to "protect" us against *E. coli* and other bacteria, it is time to understand exactly what we are biting into. Here is some food for thought from Dr. Gibbs' book which is excerpted from the first chapter entitled "Food Irradiation—The Untold Story."

Imagine, if you will, the future as envisioned by the budding food irradiation industry American families will sit down to a dinner where the bread, meat, fruit, and vegetables before them have been preserved by exposing them to nuclear radiation. The molecular structure of this food has been changed in ways that scientists are in serious disagreement as to whether human health will be harmed. At the very least, the vitamin content has been diminished. If the food contains botulism or other spoilage that would otherwise be noticeable by smell, irradiation would have eliminated the odor, allowing the consumer to be poisoned without warning. If the treated food is labelled at all, it will have a cheery, flowerlike

symbol rather than any meaningful words that inform consumers of the process to which their food has been exposed.
—Representative Douglas Bosco,
The Congressional Record, February 4, 1987.

According to a news release from *Supermarket News* (December 1, 1997) reported by my community co-op newsletter in Bozeman, Montana, President Clinton signed a new FDA reform law on November 21, 1997. Buried in the language of the law is a provision that makes irradiated foods less visible to the consumer via changes in labeling. Now, foods that have been irradiated will no longer carry the little radura symbol. Instead, "This food has been irradiated" can appear as small as the tiniest type in the ingredients listing. This is an attempt by the FDA to "encourage acceptance of irradiated foods."

Irradiation is a process whereby foods are zapped with very high doses of gamma rays from cobalt 60 and cesium 137. These two elements are nothing short of nuclear poisons. The equivalent of ten million chest X-rays is aimed at food in order to eliminate bacteria and insects. Although approved by the American Medical Association, the British Medical Association has banned irradiation on the grounds that the risks far outweigh the benefits. In fact, many years ago, Dr. John Dawson, director of the British Medical Association's Professional and Scientific Division stated that "Irradiation can also cause changes in food affecting its quality . . . We don't know enough yet to be certain that it is safe."

American consumer safety groups agree. Representatives from the environmental lobbying organization, Food and Water, believe that irradiation can actually destroy essential elements in food, including vitamins A, B complex, C, E and K. Other researchers are concerned about the effects of irradiation on amino acids, essential fatty acids and enzymes. Still others fear that irradiation will produce strains of resistant microbiological mutations. They point out that these mutated bacteria can in turn create brand new strains of pesky organisms. Last but not least, irradiation has been known to discolor meats, create unappetizing flavors in meats, dairy products and fruits and change the consistency in various kinds of produce.

It would appear that irradiation at best causes deterioration of food value and at worst may cause genetic damage to the consumer. So, why is this process still being used? The U.S. Department of Commerce admits that the use of irradiation would substantially reduce the costs of dealing with nuclear waste. The justification for irradiation seems far more commercially driven than health oriented.

In the late 1980s, Dr. Parcells was finding puzzling levels of cobalt 60 in the intestinal tracts of her students, who were unexplainably suffering from swollen glands, terrible indigestion, bloatedness and gas. She was not aware at that time that irradiation had already begun on some of our foods, especially dried spices, fruits, pork and poultry.

The Dangers of Genetically Engineered Foods

Still another threat to our food supply is the specter of genetically engineered foods. The biotech industry is experimenting with the genetic structure of our food supply attempting to improve production by enabling crops to withstand much higher levels of pesticides. This is the bioengineered plan to end world hunger: new crops that can take longer doses of pesticides, chemicals that carry their own set of dangers. According to the nonprofit educational organization, Mothers for Natural Law, the biotech industry is experimenting with the genetic structure of our food supply, attempting to improve production and end world hunger. The grim reality is that if you are not eating organic, you are probably eating genetically engineered foods every day. What's happening? Dairy products from cows are being injected with a genetically altered hormone to increase milk production, and corn, potatoes, soybeans, squash, papaya, cotton, tomatoes and canola are spliced with the DNA of bacteria and viruses. These practices pervade our American food supply, but, since they are not labeled as such, none of us can make a choice whether we will eat them or not.

Individuals have identified many problems with bioengineered foods. These include the greater probability of allergy to new species and the virtual demise of our ancestral seeds. But most of all is the right to make the choice whether or not we want to eat a tomato that has been genetically altered. At this time, unless you are eating food that is labeled certified organic, you cannot find out whether that tomato has been bioengineered. Corporations have lobbied Congress and the Clinton administration so that labeling is not required.

With the permission of Mothers for Natural Law (see Resources), I am reproducing their position paper detailing the various dangers inherent in this new technology.

The Dangers of Genetically Engineered Foods

- **Toxins.** Genetic engineering can cause unexpected mutations in an organism, which can create new and higher levels of toxins in foods. In 1989, a genetically engineered form of the food supplement tryptophan produced toxic contaminants. As a result, 37 people died, 1,500 others were permanently disabled and 5,000 others became very ill. (*The New England Journal of Medicine,* August 9, 1990)

- **Allergic reactions.** Genetic engineering can also produce unforeseen and unknown allergens in foods. Without clear and precise labeling, millions of Americans who suffer from food allergies will have no way of identifying or protecting themselves from offending foods. (*Food and Drug Administration 57 Federal Register 22987*)

- **Decreased nutritional value.** Transgenic foods may mislead consumers with "counterfeit freshness" A luscious-looking, bright red tomato could be several weeks old and of little nutritional worth. Consumers will have no way of accurately judging food quality, if the foods aren't labeled.

- **No long-term safety testing.** Time has proven herbicide and pesticide use hazardous to personal and environmental health. Now, genetic engineering is being promoted as the new harmless solution to agricultural problems. But changing the fundamental make-up of food could cause unanticipated problems, just as herbicides and pesticides have. Genetic engineering uses material from organisms that have never been part of the human food supply. Without long-term testing no one knows if these foods are safe.

- **Problems cannot be traced.** If these products remain unlabeled, our nation will be sitting on a time bomb. Without labels, our public health agencies are powerless to trace problems of any kind back to their source. The potential for tragedy is staggering.

- **Increased pollution.** Scientists estimate that plants genetically engineered to be herbicide-resistant will actually triple the amount of herbicide use. Farmers, knowing that their crops can tolerate the herbicides, will use them more liberally. Biotech claims that pesticide use will decrease are also misleading. Transgenic corn, altered to contain its own insect-killing toxin, is now registered by the EPA as a pesticide and not a vegetable at all. (*Weed Technology,* 6, 1994)

- **Unpredicted and unknown side effects.** No one knows the long-range implications of this technology. In one case, a genetically engineered bacterium, developed to aid in the production of ethanol, produced residues which rendered the land infertile. Corn crops planted on this soil grew three inches tall and fell over dead. (*The Oregonian,* August 8, 1994)

- **Threatens our entire food supply.** Insects, birds and wind can carry genetically altered seeds into neighboring fields and beyond. Once transgenic plants pollinate, genetically original plants and wild relatives can be cross-pollinated. All crops, organic and non-organic, are vulnerable to contamination from gene drift.

- **Imprecise technology.** Genetic engineering is like performing heart surgery with a shovel. Scientists don't know enough about living systems to perform DNA surgery without causing mutations and changes in the organism. They are experimenting with very delicate, yet powerful forces of nature, without full knowledge of the repercussions.

- **Gene pollution cannot be cleaned up.** Once genetically engineered organisms, bacteria and viruses are released into the environment it is impossible to contain or recall them. Unlike chemical or nuclear contamination, negative effects are irretrievable and irreversible.

- **Increased pollution of food and water supply.** Approximately 57 percent of the research of biotechnology companies is focused on the development of plants that can tolerate larger amounts of herbicides. It's estimated that this will triple the amount of herbicides used on crops, resulting in even more chemicals in our food and water. (Environmental concerns with herbicide-tolerant plants; Goldberg, *Weed Technology*, 6, 1994)

- **Genetically engineered foods do not have a clean safety record.** In 1989, a genetically engineered form of the food supplement tryptophan produced toxic contaminants. As a result, 37 people died, 1,500 others were permanently disabled, and 5,000 others became very ill. Who can guarantee that this kind of mistake won't happen again? (Eosinophilia-myalgia syndrome and tryptophan production: a cautionary tale. Mayeno, A.N., Gleich, G.J. *Tibtech*, 12, 346–352, 1994)

- **Genetic engineering may transfer new and unidentified proteins from one food into another, triggering allergic reactions.** Millions of Americans who are sensitive to allergens will have no way of identifying or protecting themselves from offending foods. Allergic reactions can cause more than simple discomfort—they can result in life-threatening anaphylactic shock. (*Food and Drug Administration 57 Federal Register 22987*)

- **Unfamiliar genetic material and gene products may be added to foods, combining in ways that are unpredictable and that permanently change the nature of our food.** The genetic structure of plants and animals has been nourishing the human race for millennia. Now that structure is being tampered with. Genes from bacteria, viruses and insects, which have never been part of the human diet, are being spliced into our food. No one really knows if they are safe. Genetic engineering is not an exact science. Scientists can unintentionally create changes in the genetic make-up of plants that result in new, unknown proteins with unknown results.

- **Genetically engineered foods may cause unexpected effects that may not be seen for years after the foods have been introduced.** Changing the fundamental make-up of a food could cause new diseases, just as herbicides and pesticides have in the past. There are no long-term studies to prove the safety of genetically engineered foods. These products are not being thoroughly tested before they arrive on the grocery shelves—they are being tested on us.

Pesticides

While concern for pesticides may seem a little tame in comparison to dangers of genetically engineered foods, there is still valid reason for concern about pesticide residues. According to Charles Benbrook, a consultant to Consumer's Union who was interviewed in the June 1997 *Nutrition Action Health Letter* published by the Center for Science in the Public Interest, "We know that prolonged exposure to pesticides raises the risk of some cancers, neurological problems like Alzheimer's and Parkinson's diseases and developmental problems. It can also weaken the immune system, which leaves us more vulnerable to disease." Benbrook went on to say that pesticide exposure can impair, block or disrupt both the development and the normal triggering of the immune system.

The same issue of *Nutrition Action* includes a list of domestic and imported produce highest in pesticide residues. The chart was prepared by the Environmental Working Group in Washington D.C. using FDA data. According to this research, the top ten most pesticide-ridden produce includes:

1. Strawberries
2. Cherries (U.S.)
3. Apples
4. Cantaloupe (Mexico)
5. Apricots
6. Grapes (Chile)
7. Blackberries
8. Pears
9. Raspberries
10. Nectarines

According to this article, "The FDA detected a total of 30 different pesticides on different batches of strawberries, for example. Seventy percent of all strawberries contained at least one pesticide and 36 percent contained two or more. Strawberries were also laced with the highest average levels of endocrine disruptors, which can mimic or interfere with hormones."

But fruits and vegetables are not the only source of harmful pesticides. Pesticides, like other toxins, are often stored in an animal's body fat, where they accumulate over time in dangerous concentrations. When they frequent polluted waters, predator fish like the striped bass and bluefish build up harmful concentrations of pesticides and other toxic chemicals in their flesh. Both herbivorous and carnivorous land animals do so also, unless they are organically raised.

Preservatives and Food Additives

Unlike most pesticides, not all food additives are bad. For example, the antioxidants vitamin E and rosemary are used as additives because they fight rancidity. But some additives frequently used in American food are truly hazardous to our health, and they must be cautioned against.

Monosodium glutamate (MSG). In people sensitive to it, this flavor enhancer causes numbness, pressure and tingling, often in the face, neck and shoulders. Because MSG is used regularly in Chinese food, these sensations are known as Chinese restaurant syndrome. MSG can also cause asthma attacks. It destroys brain cells in young mice. The FDA, however, has approved MSG as a "natural flavoring."

Nitrites. Nitrites combine with amines to form nitrosamines, which have been shown to be powerful carcinogens. As a result, the USDA has lowered the levels of nitrites permissible in processed meats but has not banned them completely. It has also mandated that ascorbic acid be added to bacon to help inhibit formation of nitrosamines. Even the most easygoing dieticians warn against eating nitrites.

Sulfites. Because of their potential to cause fatal allergy and asthma attacks in people sensitive to them, sulfites have been increasingly regulated. They are still used in food and drugs, but you will find them listed on the label as one of the following: sulfur dioxide, potassium bisulfite, metabisulfite, sodium sulfite, bisulfite or metabisulfite. Shrimps are the only food for which they may not be listed on the label. Since sulfites can be a by-product of wine fermentation, all wine labels carry a warning, even when no sulfites have been added.

Colors. Red no. 40 and yellow no. 5 are two food dyes now under fire as health risks. Various other food, drug and cosmetic (FD&C) dyes have been banned by the FDA. People are individually sensitive to those dyes that are allergens, as many appear to be.

Food Processing and Cooking

According to Dr. Paul Dudley White, M.D., "Most health problems begin in the kitchen." Food storage and cooking techniques affect vitamin and mineral loss in foods. Food cooked at very high temperatures, especially vegetables high in the B vitamins are susceptible to great nutrient loss. Even vegetables that are cut and stored for an extensive length of time, such as salad ingredients at salad bars, lose many of their nutrients. Vitamins leach into water when vegetables are boiled, which is why steaming is a better cooking technique. Basically, light, heat, extensive soaking in water and extended exposure to air are all culprits that deteriorate food quality.

The USDA believes that over 30 percent of the chicken we consume today is infected with salmonella due to our processing techniques while other researchers feel this is a modest estimate; they believe it is more like 60 percent. Is it possible that many of our so-called flu symptoms are from food poisoning rather than from a virus? It is important for us to examine our food handling techniques to make sure we aren't sabotaging our efforts to sustain ourselves.

To Microwave or Not to Microwave: That Is the Question

Well over 70 percent of our population owns a microwave and, with our fast-paced and hectic lifestyles these days, we can understand the convenience microwave cooking provides. But, is it a healthy way to cook?

I personally don't think so. My primary objection to microwave cooking is that it heats food very unevenly as anyone who has ever found a "cold spot" can tell you. Not only is the "cold spot" unappetizing, but it means that the food has not been heated enough to destroy any food-borne bacteria or parasites. This is why I believe that a microwave may not be the best method of cooking raw meat or fish.

I am also concerned about the fact that exposing food to microwaves may alter its molecular structure, especially that of proteins. We simply do not know the long-term results of this relatively new cooking method. A small Swiss study revealed some rather unexpected news about microwaved foods. In the study, eight participants ate cooked or raw food. The food that was cooked was prepared using a microwave or regular conventional cooking procedure, and the food was fed to the volunteers first thing in the morning on an empty stomach. Blood was taken before, 15 minutes following the food, and two hours later. The surprising results were that many detrimental changes were noted in the blood samples of those participants fed the microwaved meals during the two months of the study. Not only were their cholesterol levels elevated, but cell changes appeared in erythrocyte, leukocyte, hematocrit and hemoglobin values. All of these levels went down to low-normal, suggesting a marked trend toward anemia.

What You Can Do to Detoxify Your Food

Bacteria, parasites, pesticides and other contaminants can be removed from food with a Clorox bath. I use such a bath for just about all the food that I prepare at home and urge everyone else to do the same Again, as mentioned earlier in this book, Clorox is not chlorine. As a matter of fact, the active ingredient in Clorox, sodium hypochlorite, breaks down into salt and water.

The oxygenating value of the Clorox bath was discovered by Dr. Parcells while she was the head of the Nutrition Department at the Sierra States University in the 1960s. The story goes that a friend brought her a bunch of shriveled lemons. For some unknown reason, she decided to dump the lemons in water with some Clorox. Amazingly, within a half-hour the lemons regenerated and became plump once again. The entire room became filled with the fragrance of fresh lemons. Dr. Parcells surmised that the Clorox enabled the lemons to take in oxygen.

Here is the Clorox cleansing bath Dr. Parcells recommended: Add 1 teaspoon of Clorox to 1 gallon of water, being careful of the quantity of Clorox used since it is a powerful substance. To ensure quality, I use only brand-name Clorox. Place the food in the bath according to type for the following length of time.

Leafy vegetables	15 minutes
Root, thick-skinned or fibrous vegetables	30 minutes
Thin-skinned fruits, such as berries, plums, peaches, apricots	15 minutes
Thick-skinned fruits, such as citrus, bananas, apples	30 minutes
Poultry, fish, meat, eggs	20 minutes

Don't place ground meat in a Clorox bath, but frozen meat can be thawed in a Clorox bath, allowing about 20 minutes for up to five pounds of meat. Remove food from the bath and place in clear water for 10 minutes. After this rinse, dry the food thoroughly.

If you feel you have been exposed to cobalt 60 through food irradiation (as most of us are likely to be these days), detoxify yourself with a baking soda bath. Dr. Parcells suggested dissolving two pounds of baking soda in a tub of water as hot as can be tolerated. Stay in the bath until the water has cooled.

Buy food that is certified as organically grown whenever possible. Avoid all foods with preservatives, additives, coloring agents, and the radura (flower within a circle) radiation symbol.

Continue to consume those vegetables and fruits that are highest in phytochemicals, plant substances which have powerful disease prevention and healing properties. These include tomatoes, broccoli, cauliflower, cabbage, kiwi, lemons, limes, onions, garlic, flaxseed, carrots, olives and many more.

To learn more about the dangers of irradiation contact Food and Water. To learn more about the dangers of genetically engineered foods contact Mothers for Natural Law (see Resources).

11
Detoxifying Your Body:
Detox 'n Diet Plan

We've now uncovered many unsuspected sources of toxins in our outer environment ranging from the Big Four (sugar, parasites, toxic metals and radiation) to common household chemicals, cosmetics and computer screens in our home and working environment. Based upon years of personal experience and the secrets of my mentor Dr. Hazel Parcells, I have shared with you the very best ways to purify air, light, food and water. Hopefully, you have begun to make some lasting lifestyle changes step-by-step and have started to eliminate many toxins from your life so that you are not adding to your already overburdened toxic overload. Now it's time to detoxify your body.

My Detoxification Program

You can start my personal detoxification program, the Detox 'n Diet, anytime. It is a one- to four-week plan that has evolved over the past decade from my work in *Beyond Pritikin*. My clients have used it on its own several times a year or when the seasons change.

No matter what time of year you decide to begin the program, it is important that you keep warm during this procedure, because cold acts as a stressor to the system. Cold makes the body contract and thereby impedes elimination. It is also important that you have sufficient rest during the detox period since your body needs all of its energy for eliminating its accumulation of toxins.

The Detox 'n Diet is specifically designed to gently begin the cleansing process in the colon and lymphatics and to support liver function at the same time. In addition, Detox 'n Diet provides an eating plan which eliminates all processed foods, white flour, white sugar, artificial sweeteners, margarine, vegetable shortening, as well as the whole grains from wheat, rye, oats and barley, which are highly allergenic and therefore toxic to many individuals.

I personally know how absolutely wonderful you will feel after you detox. You will have more energy, more clarity, better elimination and glowing skin. You will look and feel younger. The detox program I am going to share with you has been part and parcel of my own life for the past ten years; it is the reason I can keep up with the pace of writing books and articles, traveling, lecturing, counseling and doing radio and television—a schedule that would surely exhaust anyone half my age. I firmly believe, judging from my results and those of my clients, that detoxification is the missing link to overall health and vitality. And the particular program you will be introduced to is a powerful healing therapy designed for every individual who breathes, eats and drinks in today's toxic world.

As my good friend and colleague Dr. Elson Haas once stated at a Health Sciences Symposium in San Francisco, California, "Colds, flu, cancer, cardiovascular disease, arthritis and allergens are all examples of congestive disorders which may be prevented or treated, at least in part and often dramatically, by embarking on a process of cleansing and detoxification."

There are many added benefits of this diet that go far beyond detoxification. First of all, you will be delighted to find that Detox 'n Diet is an effective stand-alone program for effortless weight loss. As a matter of fact, those of you who need to lose a good 10–20 pounds can stay on this program as long as necessary to achieve your desired results. Also, be aware that Detox 'n Diet can serve as an allergy identification program, as well. The most prominent allergenic foods—wheat, corn, dairy and yeast—are purposefully omitted from this program because weight problems are often a result of food allergies that can create water retention and water weight gain up to 5 pounds. If this program makes you feel more energetic both physically and mentally, allows you to lose water weight quickly, helps to make your puffiness or bags under the eyes disappear and enables you to experience less digestive disturbances like bloating, gas and abdominal cramps, then you know you are on the right track. Even after you have completed Detox 'n Diet, try to avoid or find substitutes for the suspected allergenic foods to avoid further allergy-induced weight gain.

Components of the Detox 'n Diet Program

You will be eating whole unprocessed foods: fresh fruits, vegetables, organically raised protein and essential fats in the form of omega-3-rich flaxseed oil and omega-6-rich gamma linolenic acid (GLA) supplements. These foods should be eaten without any seasonings (including spices, herbs, salt or vinegars and mustards) to prevent added water retention or yeast growth.

Not only are processed and refined carbohydrates and whole grains (wheat, rye, oats and barley) eliminated, but also starchy vegetables, such as acorn or butternut squash, beans, carrots, corn, parsnips, peas and potatoes. Omitting these foods, which are high on the glycemic index, will help to balance blood sugar levels so effectively that you will not be overly hungry. Detox 'n Diet also eliminates all sources of fat from the diet except for supplemental essential fatty acids, which I consider healing oils. This strategy gives the liver a well-deserved vacation from its many fat-metabolizing functions, including normalizing blood fats and manufacturing bile to digest dietary fats and oil. The program is simple to follow. It consists of these basic elements:

1. Wholesome unprocessed foods
2. Healing oils
3. A high-fiber cocktail
4. Special liver support supplements for cleansing and detoxification
5. Filtered water
6. Moderate exercise
7. Diluted unsweetened cranberry juice

Let's review these elements in detail one by one.

WHOLESOME UNPROCESSED FOODS

The food that you eat while on this plan must be organic or purified. It is essential to give the liver a rest from detoxifying pesticides and sprays. Use the Clorox bath for cleansing non-organic food, as discussed in Chapter 9.

Lean Protein. Although it may surprise you to find animal protein on a detox diet, it is absolutely essential. Remember that protein is needed to ensure that the liver can produce adequate enzymes to break down toxins into water-soluble substances for excretion. Excessive levels of carbohydrates can hinder this process. Lean beef, veal or lamb, skinless chicken or turkey and all kinds of fish can be eaten. Eat a piece about the size of the palm of your hand each day for at least two meals. The meat and poultry you eat should be organically raised and hormone-free. You may also eat whole organic eggs, since recent research has shown that eating egg whites by themselves increases susceptibility to allergy.

Vegetarians can eat tempeh or high-protein powders that are very low in carbohydrates. Try to find protein powders that contain at least 12 to 14 grams of protein per tablespoon with negligible carbohydrate and fat grams. My personal favorites which seem to be the best tolerated and least allergenic include Solgar's Whey To Go (lactose-free whey) and Naturade's Fat-Free Vegetable Protein.

Vegetables. You can eat unlimited amounts of raw or steamed vegetables that are on the lower end of the glycemic index. I recommend you choose some of the following for their high fiber content.

Asparagus	Green beans
Bamboo shoots	Lettuce
Bell peppers, green and red	Mung bean sprouts
Broccoli	Okra
Brussels sprouts	Onions
Cabbage	Parsley
Cauliflower	Radishes
Chinese cabbage	Tomatoes
Cucumber	Water chestnuts
Eggplant	Watercress
Escarole	Yellow squash
Garlic	Zucchini

Fruit. Eat fruit twice a day in moderate amounts and from the lower end of the glycemic index. The following examples will give you an idea of the kinds and amounts. Each of these equals a single serving.

1 small apple	1 small orange
10 large cherries	1 peach
½ grapefruit	2 medium plums
1 nectarine	6 large strawberries

Starting the Detox Portion of Detox 'n Diet

HEALING OILS

I have been recommending omega-3-rich flaxseed oil and omega-6-rich GLA for years. Since some Americans have been trying to live fat-free for the past decade and others have been overeating saturated and hydrogenated fats, I find that these essential healing oils are missing from most diets and need to be added. They are helpful in strengthening cell walls to protect the system against invading toxins. They also are known to alleviate arthritis, inflammatory bowel disease, kidney disease, infections, allergies, fatigue and depression. Besides these benefits, these oils can increase metabolism, attract oil-soluble poisons which have been lodged in fatty tissues of the body and carry them out of the system for elimination. For these reasons, Detox 'n Diet includes two tablespoons of flaxseed oil a day and 4–8 capsules of GLA.

HIGH-FIBER COCKTAIL

Twice a day, when you rise and when you go to bed, blend and drink eight ounces of unsweetened cranberry juice (I use Just Cranberry by Knudsen) with a teaspoon of powdered psyllium husks. The psyllium husks will soften and lift waste build-up from the intestinal walls to be carried out of the system. If you find the unsweetened cranberry juice too tart, use four ounces of juice diluted with four ounces of water.

Cranberry juice, a known cleanser of the urinary tract, contains several digestive enzymes not found in other foods and is therefore helpful for cleaning out the lymphatic system—the most underrated system in the body. Cranberry juice is a potent detoxifier of the lymphatic system, which has been called the garbage collector of the body. The lymphatic system is made up of millions of tiny channels running through all parts of the body. The lymphatic cells transport all kinds of waste products from the blood to the cells. And while blood circulation has a rhythmic flow dictated by the pumping of the heart, the lymphatics are dependent upon muscle contraction to provide their flow. They pick up all the metabolic wastes from fats and proteins and bring them to the lymph nodes for more extensive processing. The cranberry in the high-fiber cocktail helps to digest stagnated lymphatic waste. Perhaps this is why my clients swear that the high-fiber cocktail is the magic ingredient that makes their cellulite seem to disappear.

Note that due to cranberry's special fat-flushing enzymes, diluted unsweetened cranberry juice can be taken at breakfast, lunch and dinner instead of plain unfiltered water.

LIVER SUPPORT

At least twice a day you also must include a formula for optimum liver support. An ideal formula should include adequate antioxidants including glutathione and its precursors glutamine, taurine and catalase. As an alternative to these nutrients, certain herbs can also be used for their antioxidant benefits. Two of my favorite liver-protective herbs are dandelion root and milk thistle. While dandelion has a long history of use in liver disorders, the common milk thistle is also highly regarded for its ability to protect the liver. The active substance in milk thistle is called *silymarin*. Functioning as an antioxidant in and of itself, silymarin is many times more powerful than vitamin E. In addition, silymarin protects against glutathione depletion when toxic substances are present in the liver.

Resources. To make it easy for you, all the necessary supplements for success on the Detox 'n Diet program can be obtained in a Fat Flush Kit from Uni Key (see Resources). The kit is composed of a Special Dieters' Multivitamin and Mineral, GLA-90 capsules and a specific liver support formula containing milk thistle and dandelion root plus other lipotropic factors, vitamins, minerals and amino acids helpful in aiding the liver to metabolize stored fats. This formula is called the Weight Loss Formula because it is also helpful for those who wish to lose weight.

FILTERED WATER

Apart from the two high-fiber cocktails a day, try to drink only pure filtered water between meals or to dilute the unsweetened cranberry juice during meals while you're on the Detox 'n Diet program. Avoid all soft drinks, including diet sodas, coffee and tea, even herbal tea at this time. Don't drink alcohol, carbonated or mineral water, or fruit juices, even if they are unsweetened. All these beverages (including herbal tea) require processing by the body, and we want to give the body a well-deserved rest. Pure filtered water, on the other hand, dilutes toxins and cleanses them from the system.

Drinking lots of water helps flush the intestines, liver and kidneys, the organs that are involved in the detox process. I recommend drinking eight ounces of pure hot water with the juice of half a lemon twice a day, in order to help flush out the liver and kidneys. Drink another six glasses of pure water a day at room temperature. Water at room temperature interferes less with the digestive processes than either hot or cold water. Notice that I repeatedly say pure filtered water and never tap water. Refer back to the chapter "Detoxifying Your Food and Water" to choose the best method to purify water. But remember that for Detox 'n Diet, it is essential that the water you drink is filtered, because water is such a key factor in successful detoxification.

MODERATE EXERCISE

Moderate exercise will encourage bodily processes to stay active and keep toxins moving on out. Moderate exercise means taking a brisk walk for half-an-hour or spending at least 20–30 minutes a day on a NordicTrack or treadmill. Swimming, cycling and gardening are also highly recommended. The important thing is to not be sedentary.

When doing Detox 'n Diet, it is helpful to use specific lymphatic cleansing exercises. One of the most effective ways to cleanse the lymph system is to use a mini trampoline or rebounder. Simply use the mini tramp for at least five minutes a day, leaning on the balls of the feet and walking in place. Since the lymph system has no pump, this stimulates circulation in the lymph which can rid the body of toxins and waste products. Stretching exercises and yoga are also effective for stimulating lymph flow. Daily brisk walking in which you dramatically swing your arms back and forth also helps to stimulate movement in the upper lymph system. Since fasting stimulates the release of stored wastes from fatty storage deposits, it can overload the system by dumping wastes into the bloodstream too quickly and exceeding the liver's capacity for detoxification.

Based on startling research reported by Dr. Jeffrey Bland, animal studies on fasting show that after a mere 36 hours (and most cleansing juice fasts require at least 48 hours), the body becomes drained of glutathione (a primary antioxidant), enzymes and other nutrients necessary for detoxification. The antioxidant properties of glutathione are crucial during internal cleansing because the resulting metabolic by-products can damage the liver and other organs without glutathione to help break down the toxins. In addition, without the proper level of enzymes and nutrients, metabolic waste products prey upon the immune and endocrine systems.

Adequate protein intake during cleansing can also make an enormous difference in the process of detoxification. Protein activates the production of the enzymes needed to begin to break down toxic materials. As with lack of glutathione, lack of protein during cleansing can increase the production of secondary toxins and result in lower levels of glutathione. On the other hand, high levels of carbohydrates alone can depress the production of needed enzymes.

DETOX 'N DIET: A SAMPLE DAY

On rising

- High-fiber cocktail (1 tsp. psyllium husks mixed with 4 oz. unsweetened cranberry juice and 4 oz. water). Cranberry juice with all of its remarkable digestive enzymes will start to clean out those fatty globules in the lymphatics.
- Half-hour brisk walk or equivalent

Before breakfast

- 8 oz. hot water with lemon juice

Breakfast

- High-protein drink with vegetable juice*
- 2 90-mg capsules of GLA or 4 500-mg capsules of evening primrose oil
- Antioxidant and/or liver support supplementation
- Broad-spectrum multivitamin
- 8 oz. filtered water or 4 oz. unsweetened cranberry juice with 4 oz. filtered water

Midmorning

- 1 small orange

20 minutes before lunch

- 8 oz. filtered water

*1–2 Tbs. protein powder mixed in a blender with 8 oz. vegetable juice (such as Muir Glen's organic vegetable juice) or fruit (such as one peach, one apple or one small orange and 6 oz. of water). If you choose fruit, then skip the mid-morning fruit snack.

Lunch	• 4 oz. poached salmon or tempeh
	• Large green leafy salad with green onions, shredded cabbage and water chestnuts
	• 1 Tbs. flaxseed oil
	• 8 oz. filtered water or 4 oz. unsweetened cranberry juice with 4 oz. filtered water
Midafternoon	• 16 oz. filtered water
4:00 p.m.	• 2 plums or 1 peach
20 minutes before dinner	• 8 oz. filtered water
Dinner	• 4 oz. turkey burger with tomatoes and onions
	• 4 oz. steamed broccoli and cauliflower
	• Mixed sprout salad
	• 1 Tbs. flaxseed oil
	• 2 90-mg capsules of GLA or 4 500-mg capsules of evening primrose oil
	• Antioxidant and/or liver support supplementation
	• 8 oz. filtered water or 4 oz. unsweetened cranberry juice with 4 oz. filtered water
Before bed	• High-fiber cocktail

The Importance of the Liver

The liver is the most important organ in the detox system. It is responsible for the breakdown and detoxification of the increasing quantity and variety of toxic chemicals we bring into our bodies. According to noted biochemist Jeffrey Bland, Ph.D., of Seattle-based HealthComm, the liver must be able to produce a whole family of enzymes to break down toxins into water-soluble components for elimination. When the liver becomes over-loaded, the body begins to store what the liver cannot handle. In its innate wisdom, the body chooses fatty tissue as a storage site because it is metabolically less active than other tissues. For that reason, stored toxins can stay in the body, sometimes for years. Internal cleansing, if it is done correctly, can stimu-late the release of toxins lodged in fatty tissue and assist the liver and the rest of the detox organs in removing them from the body.

LIVER-SUPPORTING SUPPLEMENTS

Remember that supplements are key to the success of your program. As a by-product of the detoxification process, free radi-cals are produced in the liver. (Remember, free radicals are highly reactive molecules that roam the body creating serious tissue damage which leads to disease.) The body's major defense against free radicals are antioxidants, a group of scavenger compounds that neutralize them. Increasing intake of antioxidant nutrients, including vitamin C, vitamin E, flavonoids and selenium will pro-tect the liver and other tissues during cleansing. Sulphur-based amino acids, such as L-cysteine and N-acetyl-cysteine (NAC), are also very helpful in assisting the detox pathway in the liver to efficiently transport toxic metals and petrochemicals out of the system.

Glutathione is another powerful antioxidant found in high levels in the liver and other organs in the detox system. It is also essential for the detox system itself. When the liver is exposed to high levels of poisons, more glutathione is demanded to properly break them down. When food intake is restricted, as when fasting, glutathione is depleted, and those dangerous secondary metabolites are free to work their damage on the liver and other organs. Supplementing with glutathione directly or glutathione-sparing herbs such as milk thistle during cleansing can support both the detox process and the antioxidant system.

THE INTERNAL BATH

Many people who have gone through the program have benefited by including the internal bath or a colonic once or twice daily, morning and evening. It is recommended that you do the internal bath at least three times during the program. For the internal bath, mix 1 tablespoon blackstrap molasses in 1 quart warm water and use it for an enema. Or, if you prefer and can find a certified colon hydrotherapist in your area, a colonic is an excellent way to assist the internal cleansing process. Please refer to Chapter 4, pages 53–54 where colonics are discussed.

THERAPEUTIC BATHING

The radiation and heavy metals therapeutic baths described in Chapters 5 and 6 can be used on this program as well as the Parcells baths that are covered in the next chapter. Therapeutic bathing should be done in the evening before retiring. Use only one bath per evening and follow the directions exactly.

FOOD FOLLOWING THE PROGRAM

For the first two days after the cleansing program has been completed, it's best to refrain from eating grain-based carbohydrates, such as bread, cereals, rice and pasta. Also, avoid all sugar and pastries. Eat light meals. To satisfy hunger between meals, eat fresh green vegetables and fresh fruits in any quantity.

For a healthy maintenance diet that will continue to help keep you free of toxins, I suggest referring to my Keats Good Health Guide, *The 40-30-30 Phenomenon.* This booklet describes the best choices for protein, carbohydrates and fat. However, no matter what food plan you decide to follow, it is essential to eat only whole organically grown foods that are prepared without preservatives or additives of any kind, especially sugar. Continue to use the Clorox baths for cleansing your food, and drink only pure filtered water.

12
More Ways to Detoxify

Here are some additional ways to detoxify that are my personal favorites. They can be used all by themselves without any kind of special cleansing program or they can be incorporated into the Detox 'n Diet.

When you help your body to expel toxins which weaken, poison and disrupt its function, you are also enabling it to renew itself and build resistance in the future to toxic invaders.

1. The Parcells therapeutic baths are effective for particular kinds of toxins including radiation and heavy metals.
2. Castor oil packs, applied to the abdomen area, have been found in recent studies to improve immune function.
3. Coffee enemas are used for more efficient liver and gall bladder detoxification.
4. Bach flower remedies are specific for a variety of emotional states.

Parcells Therapeutic Baths

The therapeutic baths in this section were developed by Dr. Hazel Parcells, a pioneer of alternative medicine who managed to cure herself of "terminal" tuberculosis in the 1930s. She lived another 50 years, and died at the age of 106. In my foreword to *Live Better Longer,* a recent book by Joseph Dispenza, I was happy to acknowledge my career debt to Dr. Parcells.

Parcells therapeutic baths operate on the principle that hot bath water draws toxins from within the body to the skin surface. As the bath water grows cooler, the toxins are removed from the skin and thrown out with the water. Thus it is essential to remain in the bath until the water cools at its own speed. Pregnant women, young children, and sick people should consult a health care professional before taking these baths. Each of the four bath formulas has evolved over years of therapeutic use for particular conditions resulting from radiation, heavy metals, irradiation and viruses.

Formula 1. If air travel, a doctor or dentist's X-ray examination, a mammogram, radiation therapy or simply living within a 50-mile radius of a nuclear plant has exposed you to radiation, this is the therapeutic bath you need.

- Dissolve 1 pound of sea salt or rock salt and 1 pound of baking soda in a tub of water as hot as you can bear.
- Remain in the bath until the water is cool.
- While in the bath sip a glass of warm water into which ½ teaspoon of rock salt and ½ teaspoon of baking soda have been dissolved.
- Allow at least four hours to pass before showering.

Formula 2. A mild (or not so mild) case of metal poisoning is more common than you may realize; for example, from the aluminum in cookware, antacids or from the mercury in your silver amalgams. If you suspect that you might have metal poisoning, try this bath. The bath is also good for removing the carbon monoxide you inhale while commuting in heavy traffic. It also works well for the remnants of pesticides that often contain heavy metal residues.

- Pour 1 cup of regular Clorox bleach into a tub of water as hot as you can bear. This amount of bleach in this volume of water will not harm your skin, but do not exceed this amount.
- Remain in the bath until the water is cool.
- Allow at least four hours to pass before showering.

Formula 3. Those of us who buy our food in supermarkets can be more or less certain that we often eat food that has been irradiated by cobalt 60 to protect against *E. coli, salmonella* and other bacteria, without even knowing it. All kinds of foods are preserved with this nuclear waste material, from fruits and vegetables to grains, meats and spices. If you regularly eat food from a supermarket, try this bath.

- Dissolve 2 pounds of baking soda in a tub of water as hot as you can bear.
- Remain in the bath until the water is cool.
- While in the bath sip a glass of warm water into which ½ teaspoon baking soda has been dissolved.
- Allow at least four hours to pass before showering.

Formula 4. This all-purpose detoxifying bath is a good preventive, especially when you feel you might be coming down with something like a cold or the flu. According to Dr. Parcells, it helps build immunity by raising the acid level of your body on a cellular basis which in turn provides a biological terrain in which bacteria and viruses cannot exist.

- Pour 2 cups of unflavored apple cider vinegar into a tub of water as hot as you can bear.
- Remain in the bath until the water is cool.
- While in the bath sip a glass of warm water that contains 1 tablespoon of unflavored apple cider vinegar.
- Allow at least four hours to pass before showering.

It is important that you take only one bath per day to maximize its effectiveness. Do not mix baths together at the same time. I have found that taking one of these baths before going to bed is the best time for optimum relaxation and detoxification. You can use the downtime during sleep for regeneration. If your skin becomes dry, then apply some olive, sesame or almond oil as you step out of the tub before toweling dry.

Castor Oil Pack

Castor oil has been used as a healing oil for a variety of maladies since ancient times. At a 1992 Conference of the American Association of Naturopathic Physicians in Tempe, Arizona, it was reported that daily use of castor oil packs for a two-week period resulted in a normalizing of liver enzymes, a decrease in elevated cholesterol levels and greater energy and well-being among the research participants.

I frequently use castor oil packs as a detox therapy to stimulate the liver and gallbladder and to draw toxins from the body. My clients report a remarkable sense of well-being and tranquility while applying the castor oil pack. Since the emotion of anger is so closely tied to the liver, you may find that angry feelings you have buried start to resurface. Stay with the feelings and try to channel them constructively. When I start to experience such feelings, I try to transform them into forgiveness of others or myself.

You will need three things: 100 percent pure, cold-pressed castor oil; wool (not cotton) flannel; and a heating pad.

- Fold the wool flannel into three or four layers and soak it with castor oil.
- Put the flannel in a baking dish and heat it slowly in the oven until it becomes hot—but not hot enough to scald or injure your skin.
- Rub castor oil on your stomach, lie down, and place the hot flannel on top of your stomach.
- Seal off the flannel with Saran Wrap or a similar plastic film.
- Cover with a heating pad for one hour, keeping the flannel as hot as safely and comfortably possible.

When you finish, wash the oil from your stomach. You can keep the oil-soaked flannel sealed in Saran Wrap or place it in a ziplock plastic bag for further use, since castor oil does not become rancid as quickly as many other oils. As a gentle detox, I recommend that you use the castor oil pack once a day for three successive days, take three days off, and then use it for another three days in a row. Continue this pattern for two weeks. For those who suffer from frequent colds, infections or chronic fatigue syndrome, consider using the castor oil pack on a daily basis for two weeks.

Coffee Enema

First, consult with your health care practitioner to make sure that there are no contraindications for taking a coffee enema. This enema helps the liver and gall bladder in their detoxification processes and clears out the lower colon. The suggested procedure is one coffee enema a day for two weeks. You need a half-hour to an hour for the enema. and if coffee keeps you awake at night, take the enema early in the day. You need four items for this enema: organic coffee; an enema bag; a colon tube; and a lubricant.

The coffee must be organically grown, because commercial coffees are laced with herbicides and pesticides. You-should be able to find organic coffee in a health food store. Any enema or douche bag is usable. The colon tube should be about 30 inches long. As this may be difficult to obtain, try a hospital supply store or call Ultra Life at 800-654-8191. Instead of commercial lubricants with their chemical contents, use a natural herbal ointment, a natural oil, or even butter.

Take the enema after a bowel movement rather than before one. Daily enemas will alter your regular pattern of bowel movements. Most people take enemas while lying on an old towel or blanket on the bathroom floor. Some people bring pillows, books or magazines, and a telephone.

- Boil 1 quart of pure water (not tap water) in a glass, stainless steel or enamel container (never aluminum or Teflon-coated).

- Pour through a coffee filter containing 1 teaspoon to 4 tablespoons of ground coffee. Do not boil the coffee. The amount of coffee that you add depends on your own tolerance for caffeine. Start with a weak coffee enema rather than a strong one. Percolated coffee is also acceptable.

- Hang the enema bag no higher than two feet off the floor. Hanging it any higher causes the fluid to flow out with too much force.

- Connect the colon tube to the enema bag and seal off the tube.

- Pour the coffee into the enema bag and allow a little to pour from the end of the tube into the toilet or a container in order to clear air from the tube. This is also a good time to recheck the temperature of the coffee to make sure it's not too hot.

- Lubricate several inches of the free end of the colon tube and insert it into the rectum, while lying on your left side. The length of tubing inserted varies greatly with individuals. Never try to force the tubing in. Expect to take several enemas before you become comfortable with the procedure.

- Unseal the tube and control the flow of coffee into the colon.

- When the flow is completed, remove the colon tube or leave it in place with the valve half open to remove gas that may be in the colon.

- Gently massage your abdomen for five minutes, while lying on your left side. Do the same while lying on your back, and then on your right side.

- After 15 minutes, sit on the toilet and expel the enema. Should you wish to do so at any time before this, do not hesitate. You should never try to forcibly hold in the enema. In fact, nothing in this entire procedure should involve force or strain.

For further information, read *Achieve Maximum Health,* by my friend and colleague, David Webster, about the importance to health of colon flora and colon hydrotherapy in general.

Detoxifying the Emotions

The body-mind connection has been proven in hundreds of clinical studies. The pioneering work of Dr. Bernie Siegel, Deepak Chopra and Joan Borysenko all demonstrate that repressed emotions and painful memories can become embedded in the cells and actually make one sick. I have found that the Bach Flower Remedies represent a form of psychotherapy in a bottle. They are a non-invasive modality that addresses negative emotional states like impatience, worry, fear, anxiety and depression. The Bach Rescue Remedy is now being used in many emergency rooms all across the country to help alleviate trauma and bring people out of comas.

The Bach Flower Remedies came about through the pioneering work of Dr. Edward Bach, a Welsh homeopath, in the 1920s. He believed that since herbs possessed therapeutic benefits, flowers must also have healing powers. Over many years, Dr. Bach experimented with flowers such as impatiens, crab apple, rock rose and other plants and trees including chicory, elm, willow, walnut and beech. Eventually, after years of research, he assigned specific healing qualities to a total of 38 plant-based substances that he categorized. These 38 substances are collectively known as the Bach Flower Remedies and are still used today just as Bach originally formulated them.

As Bach wrote in his classic work *Heal Thyself,* "The prevention and cure of disease can be found by discovering the wrong within ourselves and eradicating this fault by the earnest development of the virtue which will destroy it; not by fighting the wrong, but by bringing in such a flood of its opposing virtue that it will be swept from our natures."

In my own practice, I use the Bach Flower Remedies, which were first introduced to me by Elizabeth Keeler (see Resources), with every client. Interestingly, the most common remedies I suggest for my clients, like centaury (for boundary issues and over-giving), walnut (for cutting ties to the past), impatiens (for lack of patience and irritability) and rock rose (for being hard on oneself) are the very ones that I have found so helpful for myself. I guess there is something to the saying that "like attracts like."

Here is a basic list of the Bach remedies and their suggested uses. It is reprinted with permission from *Herbs to Relieve Stress* by eminent herbalist David Hoffmann.

- AGRIMONY. Those who suffer inner torture which they try to hide behind a facade of cheerfulness. Often used as a remedy for alcoholism.

- ASPEN. Apprehension, the feeling that something dreadful is going to happen without knowing why. Anxiety for no known reason.

- BEECH. Critical and intolerant of others. Arrogant.

- CENTAURY. Weakness of will; those who let themselves be exploited or imposed upon; they have difficulty in saying "no." A human doormat.

- CERATO. Those who doubt their own judgment and intuition, always seeking the advice of others. Often influenced and misguided.

- CHERRY PLUM. Uncontrolled, irrational thoughts. Fear of losing control and doing something terrible, fear of "going crazy." Uncontrolled bursts of temper. Impulsively suicidal.

- CHESTNUT BUD. Refusal to learn by experience; continually repeating the same mistakes.

- CHICORY. Overly possessive, demands respect or attention, likes others to conform to their standards. Makes martyr of oneself. Interferes and manipulates.

- CLEMATIS. Indifferent, inattentive, daydreaming, absent-minded. Mental escapist from reality.

- CRAB APPLE. "The Cleanser Flower." Feels unclean or ashamed of ailments. Self disgust/hatred.

- ELM. Temporarily overcome by inadequacy or responsibility, though normally very capable.

- GENTIAN. Despondent. Easily discouraged and rejected. Skeptical, pessimistic. Depression, when the cause is known.

- GORSE. Desperate, without hope: "Oh, what's the use?" Defeatism.

- HEATHER. People who are obsessed with their own troubles and experiences. Talkative bores, poor listeners.

- HOLLY. For those who are jealous, envious, revengeful and suspicious. Those who hate.

- HONEYSUCKLE. For those with nostalgia who constantly dwell in the past. Homesickness.

- HORNBEAM. "Monday morning" feeling but once started, task is usually fulfilled. Mentally tired. Procrastination.

- IMPATIENS. Impatience, irritability.

- LARCH. Despondency due to lack of self-confidence; expectation of failure, so fails to make the attempt. Feels inferior, yet has the ability.

- MIMULUS. Fear of known things, fear of the world. Shyness, timidity, bashfulness.

- MUSTARD. Dark cloud of depression that descends for no known reason which can lift just as suddenly, making one downcast, saddened and low.

- OAK. Brave determined type. Struggles on in illness and against adversity despite setbacks. Plodders, never resting.

- OLIVE. Drained of energy, everything an effort. Physically fatigued.

- PINE. Feelings of guilt. Blames oneself for the mistakes of others. Feels unworthy.

- RED CHESTNUT. Excessive care of and concern for others, especially those held dear.

- ROCK ROSE. Alarmed, panicky, full of trepidation.

- ROCK WATER. For those who are hard on themselves and often overwork. Rigid, self-denying, ascetic.

- SCLERANTHUS. Uncertainty, indecision, vacillation. Fluctuating moods.

- STAR OF BETHLEHEM. For all the effects of upsetting news or fright following an accident. For release from trauma, no matter how old it is.

- SWEET CHESTNUT. Absolute dejection. Feels as if one has reached the limits of what one can stand.

- VERVAIN. Overenthusiasm, overeffort, straining. Fanatical and highly strung. Incensed and frustrated by injustices.

- VINE. Dominating/inflexible/ambitious/tyrannical/autocratic. Arrogant pride. Considered to be good leaders.

- WALNUT. Protection remedy against powerful influences; helps adjustment to any transition or change, e.g., puberty, menopause, divorce, new surroundings. Unlike Centaury the person knows what he wants, but is easily influenced by other people to do something else.

- WATER VIOLET. Proud, reserved, sedate types, sometimes feel "superior." Little emotional involvement but reliable, dependable.

- WHITE CHESTNUT. Persistent unwanted thoughts. Preoccupation with some worry or episode. Mental arguments. Constant inner dialogue.

- WILD OAT. Helps determine one's intended path of life.

- WILD ROSE. Resignation, apathy. Drifters who accept their lot, making little or no effort for improvement; lacks ambition.

- WILLOW. Resentment and bitterness with "not fair" and "poor me" attitude.

- RESCUE REMEDY. Dr. Bach combined five specific Remedies (Cherry Plum, Clematis, Impatiens, Rock Rose, Star of Bethlehem) to formulate an emergency composite that he called Rescue Remedy. Its purpose is to comfort, reassure and calm those who have received upsetting news or have experienced a trauma.

Up to six different remedies can be taken at one time. When you feel your particular condition or situation resolve, then it may be time to move on to another remedy. If you are "stuck" and are unsure of what you need, you may want to try wild oat which can help with clarity.

Letting Go

Another very helpful way to detoxify emotions is to learn how to let go, remain detached and let a greater force take over. Keep in mind that as you start eliminating toxins from your food, air and water and begin a detoxification program for your body, all those stuffed emotions in your cells, tissues and organs may start to surface for release and transformation. While meditation, yoga and deep breathing can all achieve similar "letting go" results, I personally like the following anonymous piece because it appeals to my intellectual need for inspiration and uplifting. I read it on a daily basis as a constant reminder that although I cannot understand or let alone control things, there is a greater plan operating in the world.

These are instructions on how to let go. Perhaps it is letting go of a rebellious child, or a burden of sorrow, losing a loved one or learning to live with a heartache that we just cannot let go of. Read this over . . . study it . . . pray over it . . . and you will find that letting go of your load will release a peace within you that will allow your spirit to soar.

To let go doesn't mean to stop caring; it means I can't do it
    for someone else.
To let go is not to cut myself off; it's the realization that I
    can't control another.

To let go is not to enable. but to allow learning from natural
consequences.

To let go is to admit powerlessness, which means the out-
come is not in my hands.

To let go is not to try to change or blame another; I can
only change myself.

To let go is not to care for, but to care about.

To let go is not to fix, but to be supportive.

To let go is not to judge, but to allow another to be a human
being.

To let go is not to be in the middle arranging all the outcomes, but to allow others to effect their own outcomes.

To let go is not to be protective; it is to permit another to
face reality.

To let go is not to deny, but to accept.

To let go is not to nag, scold or argue, but to search out my
own shortcomings and to correct them.

To let go is not to adjust everything to my desires, but to
take each day as it comes and to cherish the moment.

To let go is not to criticize and regulate anyone, but to try to
become what I dream I can be.

To let go is not to regret the past, but to grow and live for
the future.

To let go is to fear less and to love more.

References

Chapter 1: A New View of Aging

J. D. Beasley, *The Kellogg Report Institute of Health Policy and Practice*. The Bard College Center, 1989, p. 171.

Berney Goodman, *When the Body Speaks Its Mind*. New York: Tarcher/Putnam, 1994.

Rachel Carlson, *Silent Spring*. New York: Houghton Mifflin, 1962.

Amy E. Dean, *Natural Acts: Reconnecting with Nature to Recover Community, Spirit, and Self*. New York: Evans, 1997.

Matthew L. Wald, Danger from uranium waste grows as government considers its fate. *New York Times,* Mar. 25, 1997.

Rodney Barker, *And the Waters Turned to Blood*. New York: Simon & Schuster, 1997.

John J. Fialka, U.S. government fishes for answers to outbreak of micro-organisms hurting seafood industry. *Wall Street Journal* Oct. 9, 1997.

Chapter 3: Sugar, Toxic Invader #1

Ann Louise Gittleman, *Get the Sugar Out: 501 Simple Ways to Cut the Sugar Out of Any Diet*. New York: Crown, 1996.

Robert Atkins, M.D., *Dr. Atkins' New Diet Revolution.* New York: Evans, 1992.

Bruce Miller and James Scala, *Better Health.* Dallas, Texas: Miller Enterprises, Inc., 1994.

T. L. Cleave, *The Saccharine Disease.* New Canaan, Connecticut: Keats, 1975.

John Yudkin, *Sweet and Dangerous.* New York: Wyden, 1972.

R. A. DiFronzo, Insulin secretion, insulin resistance and obesity. *International Journal of Obesity,* 1982, 6 (Supplement I), pp. 73–82.

R. A. DiFronzo et al., Differential responsiveness of protein synthesis and degradation to amino acid availability in humans. *Diabetes* (45) 1996, April, pp. 393–7.

Barry Sears, Ph.D., *The Zone.* New York: Regan Books, 1995.

Quillin, Patrick, Ph.D., R.D., *Beating Cancer with Nutrition.* Tulsa, Oklahoma: The Nutrition Times Press, Inc., 1994.

Michael R. Eades, M.D., and Mary Dan Eades, M.D., *Protein Power.* New York: Bantam, 1996.

Russell Blaylock, *Excitotoxins: The Taste That Kills.* Santa Fe: Health Press, 1994.

Douglas Hunt, *No More Cravings.* New York: Warner Books, 1987.

Isadore Rosenfeld, Health report, *Vogue,* p. 246, April 1997.

Ann Louise Gittleman, *Beyond Pritikin.* New York: Bantam, 1996.

Chapter 4: Parasites, Toxic Invader #2

Ann Louise Gittleman, *Guess What Came To Dinner: Parasites and Your Health.* Garden City Park, New York: Avery, 1993.

———, *Parasites: The Plague of Our Times.* Baltimore, Maryland: Health Sciences Institute, 1997.

Louis Parrish, The protozoal syndrome, *Townsend Letter for Doctors,* p. 832, December 1990.

P. W. Moser, Danger in diaperland, *In Health,* p. 78, Sept.-Oct., 1991.

Robert McCabe and J. Remington, Toxoplasmosis: The time has come, *New Engl. J. Med.,* 318:313–15, February 1988.

Malaria Surveillance Annual Summary 1989, Atlanta: Centers for Disease Control, 1990.

L. Litter, Pinworms: A ten year study, *Archiv. Pediatrics,* 78:440–55, November 1961.

C. Lane et al., If your uneaten food moves, take it to a doctor, *JAMA,* 260:340, July 15, 1988.

J. McKerrow et al., Anasakiasis: Revenge of the sushi parasite, *New Engl. J. Med.,* 319:1228, Nov. 3, 1988.

Karen Vanderhoof-Forschner, *Everything You Need to Know About Lyme Disease and Other Tick-Borne Disorders.* New York: Wiley, 1997.

D. Lang, *Coping with Lyme Disease.* 2d ed., New York: Owl/Holt, 1997.

Chapter 5: Heavy Metals, Toxic Invader #3

Arthur C. Upton and Eden Graber (eds.), *Staying Healthy in a Risky Environment: The New York University Medical Center Family Guide.* New York: Simon & Schuster, 1993.

Richard Casdorph, M.D. and Morton Walker. *Toxic Metal Syndrome.* Garden City Park, New York: Avery, 1995.

Paul C. Eck and Larry Wilson, *Toxic Metals in Human Health and Disease.* Phoenix: Eck Institute of Applied Nutrition and Bioenergetics, 1989.

Tru Temp Health System Cookware Insert, *Health Sciences Institute,* 2(5) November 1997.

Jerome O. Nriagu. *Lead and Lead Poisoning Antiquity.* New York: John Wiley & Sons, 1983.

Debra J. Brody et al., Blood lead levels in the U.S. population, *JAMA,* 272:277–83, 1994.

Strategic Plan for the Elimination of Childhood Lead Poisoning, Atlanta: Centers for Disease Control, 1991.

Irene Kessel and John T. O'Connor, *Getting the Lead Out: The Complete Resource on How to Prevent and Cope with Lead Poisoning.* New York: Plenum, 1997.

Carey Goldberg, Colleagues vow to learn from chemist's death, *New York Times,* Oct. 3, 1997.

Robert L. Siblerud et al., Psychometric evidence that mercury from silver dental fillings may be an etiological factor in depression, excessive anger, anxiety. *Psychological Reports.* 1994, Vol. 74, 67–80.

Hal A. Huggins, *Serum Compatibility Testing: A Crucial Methodology for Modern Dentistry.* Colorado Springs, Colorado: Huggins Diagnostics, Inc., 1989.

———, *It's All in Your Head: The Link Between Mercury Amalgams and Illness.* Garden City Park, New York: Avery, 1993.

Thomas Levy, *Extraordinary Science.* April-June, 1994.

Ralph Golan, *Optimal Wellness.* New York: Ballantine Books, 1995.

Chapter 6: Radiation, Toxic Invader #4

Sara Shannon, *Diet for the Atomic Age.* Garden City Park, New York: Avery, 1987.

Joseph Dispenza, *Live Better Longer: The Parcells Center Seven Step Plan for Health and Longevity.* Harper San Francisco, 1997.

Arthur C. Upton and Eden Graber (eds.), *Staying Healthy in a Risky Environment: The New York University Medical Center Family Guide.* New York: Simon & Schuster, 1993.

Jay M. Gould, *The Enemy Within: The High Cost of Living Near Nuclear Reactors.* New York: Four Walls Eight Windows, 1996.

Blanche Wiesen Cook, Cold war fallout, *The Nation,* Dec. 9, 1996.

Matthew L. Wald, Caught between risks of haste and hesitation, *New York Times,* Sept. 29, 1997.

Gerald P. Murphy, Lois B. Morris, and Dianne Lange for the American Cancer Society, *Informed Decisions: The Complete Book of Cancer Diagnosis, Treatment, and Recovery.* New York: Viking, 1997.

Steven R. Schecter, N.D., *Fighting Radiation with Foods, Herbs and Vitamins.* Brookline, Massachusetts: East West Health Books, 1988.

Chapter 7: Detoxifying Your Indoor Air Environment

Ann Louise Gittleman, Series of articles, *Natural Lifestyling,* Albuquerque, New Mexico, Dec. 1993–Sept. 1994.

Nina Anderson and Albert Benoist, *Your Health and Your House: A Resource Guide.* New Canaan, Connecticut: Keats, 1994.

Arthur C. Upton and Eden Graber (eds.), *Staying Healthy in a Risky Environment: The New York University Medical Center Family Guide.* New York: Simon & Schuster, 1993.

Mary Kearney Levenstein, *Everyday Cancer Risks.* Garden City Park, New York: Avery, 1992.

Bill Wolverton, Ph.D., *How to Grow Clean Air: 50 Houseplants that Purify Your Home or Office.* New York: Penguin, 1997.

Lily Casura, Rx for winter health: breathe green air, "clean air plants" and winter indoor air quality. *Townsend Letter for Doctors and Patients,* December 1997, pp. 68–74.

Chapter 8: Detoxifying Your Indoor Light Environment

Ann Louise Gittleman. Let there be light. *Natural Lifestyling,* Albuquerque, New Mexico, June 1994.

John Nash Ott, *Health and Light.* Old Greenwich, Connecticut: The Devin-Adair Co, 1988.

———, *Light, Radiation, and You.* Old Greenwich, Connecticut: The Devin-Adair Co., 1990.

Brian Breiling, Ph.D., and Bethany ArgIsle (eds.), *Light Years Ahead.* Berkeley, California: Celestial Arts, 1996.

Chapter 9: Detoxifying Your Water

Ann Louise Gittleman, Water: Your chemical cocktail, *Natural Lifestyling,* May 1994.

Speiser, Roy, Dr., Toxins on tap. *Explore!,* 1994 11(4):4.

Julian Whitaker, *Health & Healing,* 6(8):4–5, August 1996.

B. A. Cohen and E. D. Olsen, *Victorian Water Treatment Enters the 21st Century: Public Health Threats from Water Utilities' Ancient Treatment and Distribution Systems.* New York: Natural Resources Defense Council, 1994.

Thomas Levy, Fluoridation: Paving the road . . . to the final solution, *Extraordinary Science,* Jan./Mar., 1994.

John Yiamouyiannis, *Fluoride: The Aging Factor.* Delaware, Ohio: Health Action Press, 3d ed., 1993.

Leo Galland, *The Four Pillars of Healing.* New York: Random House, 1997.

Larry Laudan, *Danger Ahead: The Risks You Really Face on Life's Highway.* New York: Wiley, 1997.

Arthur C. Upton and Eden Graber (eds.), *Staying Healthy in a Risky Environment: The New York University Medical Center Family Guide.* New York: Simon & Schuster, 1993.

Chapter 10: Detoxifying Your Food

Arthur C. Upton and Eden Graber (eds.), *Staying Healthy in a Risky Environment: The New York University Medical Center Family Guide.* New York: Simon & Schuster, 1993.

Cover Story, *Newsweek,* April 25, 1994.

Duff Wilson. Fear in the fields: how hazardous wastes become fertilizer. *Seattle Times,* July 3, 4 and 13, 1997.

Gary Gibbs, D. O., *The Food that Would Last Forever.* Garden City Park, New York: Avery, 1993.

"Meat Irradiation Is Not the Answer." *Delicious!* December 1997:14.

"How to Avoid Pesticides." *Nutrition Action* 24(5), June 1997:1, 4–7.

Russell Blaylock, M.D., *Excitotoxins: The Taste That Kills.* Santa Fe: Health Press, 1994.

Swiss microwave study. *Spectrum,* Spring 1996.

Chapter 11: Detoxifying Your Body

Ann Louise Gittleman, *Beyond Pritikin.* New York: Bantam, 1996.

Elson Haas, M.D., *The Detox Diet.* Berkeley, California: Celestial Arts, 1996.

J. S. Bland. "Food and nutrient effects on detoxification." *Townsend Letter for Doctors and Patients,* December, 1995.

————— et al., "Nutritional upregulation of hepatic detoxification enzymes," *Journal of Applied Nutrition,* Vol. 3–4:2–15, 1992.

D. B. Mowrey, *Herbal Tonic Therapies.* New Canaan, Connecticut: Keats, 1993.

Chapter 12: More Ways to Detoxify

Joseph Dispenza, *Live Better Longer: The Parcells Center Seven-Step Plan for Health and Longevity.* HarperSan Francisco, 1997.

Deborah Seymour Taylor, Edgar Cayce on health & beauty, *Explore!,* 1997, 8(3):52–53.

Christiane Northrup, *Women's Bodies, Women's Wisdom.* New York: Bantam, 1994.

David Webster, *Achieve Maximum Health: Colon Flora—The Missing Link in Immunity, Health and Longevity.* Cardiff, California: Hygeia, 1995.

HealthExcel Programmes Body Detoxification Information Pak, Winthrop, Washington: Healthexcel, Inc., 1996.

Resources

Uni Key Health Systems
Bozeman, MT
1-800-888-4353
For parasite products, fat flush kits, the elimination formula, flora balance, radiation formula, hair analysis services and other specialty products

MannaCleanse

Mannatech, Inc.
Coppell, TX
http://independentlyhealthy.com

Chelation Therapy

To find a physician who chelates, call:
American College for Advancement in Medicine
Laguna Hills, CA
714-583-7666

Lead-testing Kit

Send a self-addressed stamped envelope to:
China Brochure
Environmental Defense Fund
P.O. Box 96969 Dept. PVN
Washington, DC 20090

For Information on Mercury-free Dentists and Serum Compatibility Testing

Peak Energy Performance˙
Colorado Springs, CO
1-800-331-2303

Bio-Electric Shields

1-800-217-8673

Radon Information

Environmental Protection Agency
1-800-SOS-RADON

Full Spectrum Lights

Duro-Test Corporation
9 Law Drive
Fairfield, NJ 07007
1-800-289-3876
Producers of Vita-Lite full-spectrum fluorescent light tubes

Light Energy Company
1056 NW 179th Place
Seattle, WA 09177
1-800-LIGHT-CO
National distributor for Ott-Lite Systems Inc.

Environmental Lighting Concepts, Inc.
3923 Coconut Palm Drive
Tampa, FL 33619
(813) 621-0058
1-800-842-8848
Distributors of Ott-Lite capsulite bulbs, full-spectrum light boxes and John Ott's total-spectrum sunglasses

The Sunbox Company
19217 Orbit Drive
Gaithersburg, MD 20879
1-800-LIGHT-YOU
Distributors of full-spectrum light boxes, dawn simulators and light visors

Bio-Brite, Inc.
7315 Wisconsin Avenue
Bethesda, MD 20814
1-800-621-LITE
Producers of Bio-Brite Light Visor

For more information regarding phototherapy, education and products:

Light Years Ahead
P. O. Box 174
Tiburon, CA 94920
(415) 435-1578

CARE 2000 Air Purification System and
Doulton Water Filters

Clean Water Revival
1-800-444-3563 or
Uni Key Health Systems
(see page 191)

Water Conditioning

GMX International
Chico, CA
(909) 627-5700

Food Safety Issues

Mothers for Natural Law
P.O. Box 1177
Fairfield, IA 52556
(515) 472-2908

Food and Water
1-800-EATSAFE

Bach Flower Remedies

Elizabeth Keeler
1-800-417-5217

Index